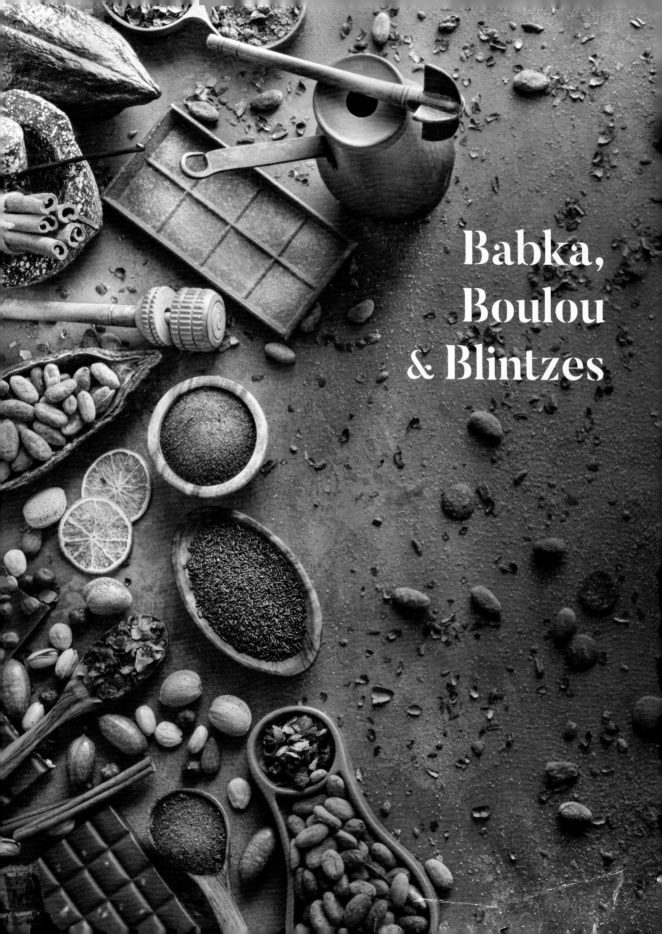

Babka, Boulou & Blintzes

Babka, Boulou & Blintzes

Jewish Chocolate Recipes from Around the World

Compiled by Michael Leventhal

Green
Bean
Books

Dedicated to Kenneth Teacher,
who loved companionship, conversation and chocolate.
Especially Sachertorte after a good day's skiing.

**Green
Bean
Books**

First published in the UK in 2021 by Green Bean Books
c/o Pen & Sword Books Ltd.
47 Church Street, Barnsley, South Yorkshire, S70 2AS
www.greenbeanbooks.com

Introduction © Michael Leventhal, 2021

Hardback edition: 9781784386993
EBook edition: 9781784387006

Edited by Anne Sheasby
Designed and typeset by Ian Hughes – www.mousematdesign.com
Cover composite and image post-production by Marc Gerstein
Picture acquisition and art direction by Judi Rose
Printed and bound in India by Replika Press Pvt Ltd.

Contents

Introduction

Why Chocolate Matters to the Jewish Community

Chocolate matters. Every day, more than a billion people worldwide enjoy chocolate and every year, over three million tons of cocoa beans are harvested.

But did you know that Jewish traders have played a key role in the chocolate industry for more than 500 years? The Jewish community has a love of food and – despite chocolate having no set part in any festivals or rituals – Jews have been crucial in helping introduce chocolate to a great many countries around the world.

Maya and Aztec

The Maya became the first to unlock the secrets of the cocoa bean more than 5,000 years ago. They dried and ground the beans, mixing them with water to create a hot, frothy chocolate drink. They even made pots with spouts and poured the liquid between them to create a cappuccino-like foam. After the Maya culture collapsed, the Aztecs followed. They believed that chocolate was a gift from the gods that was more valuable than gold. According to one report the Aztec emperor Montezuma drank more than fifty cups of hot chocolate every day.

It wasn't until 1502 that Europeans were introduced to chocolate, when Christopher Columbus made his fourth voyage to the Americas. Columbus received a gift of cocoa beans from the island of Guanaja off the coast of Honduras – but he mistakenly thought they were almonds or goat's droppings and had no idea how to use them. There are many historians who suggest Christopher Columbus himself was Jewish and there is certainly good evidence that he had Jewish ancestry. So, arguably, this is the point at which Jewish involvement in chocolate history and trade begins.

It also seems likely that a few of Columbus's crew members were Jewish. The Nazi-hunter Simon Wiesenthal spent years researching the history of Columbus's voyages and claimed in his book *Sails of Hope: The Secret Mission of Christopher Columbus* that as many as one-third of his 120-strong crew could have been Jewish. It is more likely, however, that only three of his crew were *conversos* – Jews pretending to have converted to Christianity to avoid persecution: the ship's surgeon, Maestro Bernal; Marco, a cook; and a Hebrew and Arabic interpreter named Luis de Torres.

Additionally, Columbus almost certainly received funding from two *conversos* named Louis de Santangel and Gabriel Sanchez (Gabriel's relative Rodrego Sanchez may have travelled with Columbus). He also had financial support from a well-known rabbi named Don Isaac Abarbanel.

Christopher Columbus

Spanish Conquistadores

If Columbus failed to realise the potential of his cocoa beans, Europeans didn't have long to wait for their first hit of chocolate.

In 1528, ten years after the bloody Spanish conquest of the Aztecs, some of the Aztecs' treasured chocolate – nicknamed 'brown gold' – was taken back to Spain by the Spanish conquistador Don Hernán Cortés. By the 1580s, regular imports of cocoa beans had begun because by then the Spanish had mastered the technique of converting the pods into a thick, delicious drink.

It was now that Jewish traders in Spain started playing a key role in the creation and expansion of the chocolate market. At the time they were blocked from numerous occupations as a result of widespread anti-Semitic prejudice: the chocolate business was something the Jews were able and permitted to do and so they embraced it, though trading rights were often withdrawn if they became too successful.

An aristocratic chocolate party, or *xocolotada*, in eighteenth-century Spain

France and Bayonne

Following the establishment of the Spanish Inquisition, many Spanish and Portuguese Jews were forced to flee to new countries and a number took with them the skill of chocolate-making, something they subsequently came to rely on for their livelihood.

Take the southern French town of Bayonne, which is still known as the 'chocolate capital of France'. Thanks to its riverside location, Bayonne became cocoa central after the arrival of Spanish Jews in the early 1600s; documents show that at least 60 Jewish *converso* families lived in the district of Saint Esprit.

Their chocolate became increasingly popular but Jewish chocolate makers were forced to leave Bayonne each evening before sunset. They were not allowed to establish premises or live in the city and had to carry their heavy cocoa-grinding equipment to and from houses and shops.

As time went on, many professional French and Spanish Jewish bakers introduced chocolate fillings and started making chocolate cakes – the recipe for one of those cakes is included in this collection.

Sadly, though, the Jews' success turned to their disadvantage, provoking resentment and restrictions. The Bayonnais even fought to ban Jews from making chocolate – once they had learned the craft themselves.

A series of laws was passed in the 1720s, forbidding Jews to make chocolate in shops and warehouses in Bayonne. Records show that, twenty years later, a Jewish man was caught making the drink in an apartment, and he gamely protested that the laws did not apply to apartments. In 1762 a guild of chocolate-makers was formed by Christian artisans as another attempt to block Jewish entrepreneurs from competing in the trade. By 1860, there were only two Jewish artisans left in Saint Esprit practising chocolate-making, but in Bayonne there were still 32 chocolate-makers – a very large number for a fairly small town.

Today, however, Bayonne is proud of its chocolate heritage and the city's tourist board and chocolate museums give full credit to the Jewish community. A trip, with plenty of tastings, is recommended.

As in France, Jews fleeing from the Spanish Inquisition seeded the magic of chocolate-making, and its possible fortunes, around other parts of Europe including Denmark, Holland, Portugal and England.

In Belgium, for example, the abbot of Baudelo in Ghent is believed to be the first person to take chocolate to the country in 1635 – but it was a Jewish immigrant named Emmanuel Soares de Rinero, who had settled in the province of Brabant, who was the first to be issued with a licence to manufacture chocolate.

British Coffee and Chocolate Houses

The first British coffee house to be documented as serving hot chocolate also has a strong Jewish link. This was in 1650, in the city of Oxford – a year when Jews were being readmitted to England.

According to a number of sources – including the diarist Samuel Pepys – The Angel was set up by a Lebanese Jewish entrepreneur named Jacob. His surname is not known and the date of his very first hot chocolate was not recorded. The Grand Café on the city's High Street commemorates the site today. Jacob later moved his trade to London's Holborn area, though a Frenchman had already opened the capital's first chocolate house in Bishopsgate in 1657, after which many chocolate houses quickly popped up.

Expansion Worldwide

As well as the Jewish community, other religious groups were heavily involved in the global chocolate trade. The Catholic Church encouraged the drinking of chocolate for sustenance on the numerous fasting days, while chocolate companies run by practising Quakers included Cadbury of Birmingham, Fry's of Bristol and Rowntree's of York. Richard Cadbury, the elder of the two famous Cadbury brothers, made two trips to Jerusalem in the late 1800s.

The Jewish involvement in the trade has been discussed in comprehensive detail by Rabbi Debbie Prinz in her book, *On The Chocolate Trail: A Delicious Adventure Connecting Jews, Religions, History, Travel, Rituals and Recipes to the Magic of Cacao.*

Here, I will simply set down a brief summary of the next stage in Jewish chocolate production worldwide. For that, we travel across the seas to the French Caribbean.

A Jew from Bayonne named Benjamin D'Acosta de Andrade arrived on the island of Martinique

Richard Cadbury, in the middle with a snowy beard, by the Dead Sea *c* 1897.

in 1654. D'Acosta de Andrade cultivated cacao trees and became the first person to open a cocoa-processing plant in this French territory. Other Jews soon followed his example and helped the chocolate trade develop and flourish over the next few decades.

By 1684, chocolate was Martinique's most lucrative export but by now the Jews' success had generated envy from competitors – the following year a law known as the Code Noir was published, calling for the expulsion of Jews from all French islands. So, again, the Jews were sadly not rewarded but instead forced to flee to new homes.

D'Acosta de Andrade left for the Dutch haven of Curaçao which consequently developed a thriving chocolate industry of its own. Records suggest that at least 200 Jewish cocoa brokers were working in Curaçao in the seventeenth and eighteenth centuries. In Curaçao today, hot chocolate and panlevi sponge cookies are still served at a *brit milah*, or circumcision. Recipes for both are included in this collection.

Emmanuel Israel Synagogue, Curaçao

Americas

When it comes to chocolate's arrival in North America, we can thank the well-respected Sephardi entrepreneur Aaron Lopez. He was one of the wealthiest Spanish Jews to start a successful business in the seaside city of Newport, Rhode Island.

Lopez's parents were members of the *converso* community in Lisbon, Portugal. After he arrived in Rhode Island in October 1752 he quickly became one of the city's most important merchants. Lopez was involved in many trades – shoes, hats, handkerchiefs, candles, bottles, and more – and he became one of the key people responsible for bringing the chocolate business to America by importing cocoa and producing chocolate.

Other Jewish businessmen also played an important role in the chocolate trade. Celia D. Shapiro, co-author of *Chocolate: History, Culture, and Heritage,* suggests that Jews who settled in New York were not allowed to work in retail trades but the import business was something they were permitted to do. They had connections with Dutch colonies and cacao was a profitable, viable commodity to import.

Sachertorte

It was around 1850 that a pastry maker really turned the world of chocolate baking on its head, inventing something that is still popular today – the world-famous chocolate cake known as the Sachertorte.

In a detailed blog piece Nino Shaye Weiss explains that Franz Sacher was the pastry chef responsible and writes that he was one of a long line of Central European Jewish pastry professionals. Countless other websites include the assertion that Sacher was Jewish. The claim possibly first appeared in Gil Mark's *Encyclopaedia of Jewish Food* and has been endlessly repeated – but, in fact, although his daughter-in-law was Jewish, there is no hard evidence that Sacher himself was. Also, contrary to popular belief, the cake was not developed in 1832 and it was not created in Vienna, but in Pressburg (today's Slovak capital Bratislava). One giveaway is that the 'conching' processes needed to make smooth-melting chocolate for the glossy topping of the cake were only available from the second half of the nineteenth century.

Sacher himself insisted in an interview given on the occasion of his ninetieth birthday that he first made Sachertorte around 1850 in Pressburg where he worked for the nobility at the local casino. Nino Weiss's tempting version of the cake is included here.

Franz Sacher

Chocolate Gelt

At the top of this introduction, I said that chocolate plays no set key role in any festivals or rituals. While this is true, many families around the world purchase pouches of chocolate-wrapped coins as part of their Chanukah celebrations. It's become known as Chanukah chocolate *gelt* (money in Yiddish). The tradition is believed to have been started in America by the Loft company of New York in the 1920s (when Loft Inc. was perhaps the world's largest confectionery business). It was a development from the idea of minting coins to celebrate the Macabees' military victory, and also the more recent eighteenth-century tradition of giving religious teachers money as a token of gratitude.

World War II

As the storm clouds of the Second World War gathered in Europe, the rise of the Third Reich prompted a Latvian Jewish chocolate maker, Eliyahu Fromenchenko, to emigrate to pre-state Israel in 1933. He took with him equipment from his former chocolate and sweet factory and founded the iconic Israeli company, Elite, with a factory in Ramat Gan. Elite later became the official supplier of chocolate to the Allied units stationed in Palestine during World War II.

The Nazi rule also prompted an Austrian Jewish chocolatier named Stephen Klein to escape to New York in 1939. The following year he founded the successful chocolate company, Barton's Bonbonniere, which is now known as Barton's Candy.

During World War II itself, chocolate had an unexpected role to play with a new Jewish connection. Explosives disguised as expensive chocolate bars were designed by the Third Reich as part of a curious plot to kill Winston Churchill. The Germans planned to smuggle booby-trapped bars into the Prime

The Elite Chocolate Factory, Ramat Gan

Minister's War Cabinet dining room. They intended to use secret agents based in Britain to place the elegantly wrapped 'Peter's Chocolate' bars in the dining room. A few seconds after the chocolate was removed from the packaging, the slab would detonate.

The attempt on Churchill's life was partly foiled by the Jewish scientist Lord Victor Rothschild, who was working for the security services. Rothschild asked an artist named Laurence Fish to draw up posters of the chocolate and warn the public to watch out for the bars.

Sir Winston Churchill

Chocolate and Wisdom

Some recent studies have claimed that chocolate helps improve the flow of blood to your brain as well as reducing anxiety levels. According to research published in the *New England Journal of Medicine* the countries where chocolate consumption is highest even have the most Nobel Prize recipients!

Anyone looking for further evidence of a link between chocolate and genius should look to the collection of New York's Leo Baeck Institute. It includes two porcelain and gold-leaf cups from the 1880s that were used for drinking hot chocolate by Albert Einstein and his sister Maya when they were children. The specially-commissioned cups have photos of the siblings on the side.

Albert Einstein's chocolate cup

And, in one final link to chocolate, Einstein was working as a clerk in the patent office in Berne, Switzerland, when the makers of Toblerone submitted an application for a patent – but it is not known (and seems unlikely) that it was him who approved their application.

Conclusion

In modern times, the relationship between the chocolate trade and the Jewish community is no longer as strong as it once was, but it is a shame to think that the enterprising association that existed over hundreds of years is in danger of being forgotten. So, the next time you take a bite of a bar, or enjoy a sip of hot chocolate, give a thought to the 500-year journey of this marvellous 'brown gold'.

MICHAEL LEVENTHAL, 2021

About This Collection

Five years ago, soon after becoming a father for the first time, I started publishing Jewish children's books. Then, after a trip to Bayonne in France and reading about Jewish chocolate history, I decided to try to write my own children's book on the subject. This chocolate cookbook felt like a natural extension of that story book. Over nine months I gathered a wonderful range of recipes from cooks, chefs and writers around the world. I also appealed to volunteers to pitch in and test each recipe. The aim was to raise money for Chai Cancer Care – all profits from the sale of this book will go towards supporting their work.

The subtitle of this book is 'Jewish Chocolate Recipes from Around the World' – but what makes a recipe a *Jewish* recipe? The question has been debated at numerous events and there is no definitive answer.

Some of the recipes included in this collection – such as babka and rugelach – are closely associated with the Jewish community. They are connected with particular Jewish traditions and are well-known and commonly used by Jewish cooks. There are also recipes that require ingredients like mahlab and tahini that are used in Middle Eastern cookery and arguably have a Jewish flavour – though that is not to say that they are used exclusively in Jewish cookery.

Finally, my aim was to collect and present varied recipes from Jewish cooks around the world. This collection includes mouth-watering ideas from Curaçao, Israel, Egypt, France, Germany, Hungary, Italy, the Netherlands, America, Turkey and other countries.

A year ago, a friend of my wife Rachel dropped off a delicious surprise – a batch of freshly-baked brownies. They came with a note saying, 'There are few situations which cannot be improved with a little chocolate.' I agree entirely and I hope you find plenty in this book to interest and inspire you.

Michael Leventhal

Chai Cancer Care

At Chai, we have always recognised the importance of nutrition and making informed choices. And amongst us all who can resist chocolate? So it's wonderful to know that dark chocolate enjoyed in moderation has powerful antioxidant activity!

With delicious recipes from around the world, *Babka, Boulou & Blintzes* is not just a dessert cookbook. In it you will find an eclectic and tantalising range of sweet and savoury recipes for every occasion, from sourdough rye brownies and chocolate and roasted beet ice cream to Sicilian caponata and chocolate chilli.

So many of us are touched by cancer in some way and for more than 30 years, Chai has been an essential part of our community. At the time of printing this book, we are currently supporting just over 3,600 cancer patients, their families and friends from 11 centres across the UK, in clients' own homes and internationally through Zoom, Skype and telephone counselling.

Currently, Chai provides 65 specialised services including counselling for families, individuals and couples; complementary therapies; children, teenage and family service; home support services; group activities and support groups; and the Medical Outpatient Rehabilitation and Palliative Care Service.

Chai does not receive any statutory funding and we rely on our generous donors to raise our annual running cost of £3.4 million. We are therefore extremely grateful that all proceeds from *Babka, Boulou & Blintzes* will go directly towards ensuring that Chai can continue to make such a difference to people's lives. It is fundraising ventures such as this that enable us to develop new services, meeting our clients' evolving needs.

On behalf of everyone at Chai, our heartfelt thanks to Michael for all your commitment and dedication to this fabulous project. Your loyal support means a tremendous amount to us all.

Happy cooking!

Louise Hager

Lisa Steele

Chairman

Chief Executive

Cookies, Bars
& Brownies

Kenden Alfond
Vegan Nutty Chocolate Chip Cookies

Introducing the ultimate Passover cookie! A healthier and delicious vegan chocolate chip cookie recipe that is also kosher for Passover. Make two or three batches, depending on how many guests you'll be hosting.

Makes: 12 cookies • **Prep time:** 20 minutes • **Cook time:** 20–24 minutes

230g/8oz/1¼ cups cooked/canned white beans (such as cannellini beans) or 280g/10oz/1¼ cups cooked (cooled) sweet potato purée (depending on which you eat during the Passover holiday)
60g/2¼oz/¼ cup natural almond butter
1 tsp vanilla extract
2 tbsp light or dark soft brown sugar
1 tsp baking powder
¼ tsp salt
70g/2½oz/½ cup almond flour or matzo meal
3 tbsp chocolate chips (use a dairy-, nut- and soy-free vegan version)

1. Preheat the oven to 180°C/160°C fan/350°F/Gas Mark 4. Line two baking sheets with non-stick baking paper.

2. If you are using cooked/canned white beans, rinse them well in a colander, then tip into a bowl and mash until smooth. If you are using sweet potato purée, make sure it is cool.

3. Put the mashed white beans or sweet potato purée, the almond butter, vanilla, sugar, baking powder and salt into a food processor. Process until very smooth, scraping down the sides of the bowl a couple of times. Alternatively, beat the ingredients together really well in a mixing bowl until combined (you might need to leave the almond butter at room temperature to soften it a little first).

4. Transfer the processed mixture to a mixing bowl and fold in the almond flour or matzo meal and chocolate chips until combined.

5. Place rounded tablespoonfuls of the mixture about 5cm/2in apart on the lined baking sheets.

6. Bake for about 20–24 minutes or until they turn golden brown.

7. Remove from the oven, transfer the cookies from the baking sheets to a wire rack, then leave them to cool completely before serving.

8. These will keep in an airtight container in the fridge for up to a week.

Michelle Eshkeri
Sourdough Rye Brownies

Rye has an affinity with chocolate, evidenced by various bakeries across the world making incredibly delicious brownies and cookies using both of these ingredients. The first time I came across the combination was in Claire Ptak's Violet Bakery cookbook some years ago, which is the basis for this recipe, and what struck me about using rye flour was that the danger of failure was vastly reduced; it was a dislike of dry brownies that had more or less put me off making them at all.

If you ignore the peculiar colour of egg fermenting with rye flour and proceed to the end, you will find these brownies a fudgy, sweet and lightly-fermented addition to your brownie repertoire and a good use of any spare rye starter – you could use old starter here, too, instead of making it according to the refreshment schedule below.

Makes: 12 brownies • **Prep time:** 25 minutes, plus several hours resting • **Cook time:** 35–45 minutes

Stage 1: Refreshment
72g/2½oz/½ cup
 wholegrain rye flour
57g/2oz/scant 4 tbsp water
36g/1¼oz rye or wheat
 starter (8–12 hours after
 last refreshment)

Stage 2: First mix
194g/6¾oz/1½ cups
 wholegrain rye flour
250g/9oz/5 medium eggs,
 beaten
100g/3½oz/½ cup caster or
 granulated sugar

Stage 3: Final mix
195g/6¾oz/generous
 ¾ cup unsalted butter
475g/1lb 1oz/2¾ cups dark
 chocolate (at least 66%
 cocoa solids), broken
 into pieces
77g/2¾oz/⅓ cup caster or
 granulated sugar
265g/9½oz/generous
 1¼ cups dark soft brown
 sugar

1. Place all the stage 1 ingredients in a 300ml/½ pint/1¼ cups jar or container with a lid, mix, cover and leave at warm room temperature for 4–6 hours.

2. Place all the stage 2 ingredients, plus 125g/4½oz of the starter (stage 1), in a large bowl, stir well with a whisk, cover and leave in a warm place for 1–2 hours, or more time if it suits you. It won't rise much but you should see some bubbles as evidence of fermentation on the surface of the mix.

3. In the hour before you plan to do stage 3 and bake, melt the butter and chocolate for stage 3 in a heatproof bowl set over a pan of gently simmering water (ensuring the bottom of the bowl doesn't touch the water). Remove the bowl from the pan and set aside to cool for 30 minutes.

4. Preheat the oven to 160°C/140°C fan/325°F/Gas Mark 3. Line a 25cm/10in square cake tin with non-stick baking paper.

5. Add the melted chocolate and butter, plus the remaining stage 3 ingredients, into the bowl with the stage 2 batter. Whisk until well combined. Pour into the tin and smooth the top with the back of a spoon so it is evenly distributed.

6. Bake for 30–40 minutes until the top looks dry but it still has a slight wobble. It's difficult to over-bake these.

7. Remove from the oven and sprinkle with additional sea salt, if you like, then leave to cool in the tin. When cool, cut into 12 squares to serve.

8. These will keep in an airtight container at room temperature for up to a week.

70g (2½oz/¾ cup) good-quality unsweetened cocoa powder
5g (⅛oz) vanilla extract
3g (⅛oz) bicarbonate of soda
2g (⅟₁₆oz) sea salt, plus extra (optional) for sprinkling

Tester's Tip:
● As an alternative to sea salt you can dust the top with a little cocoa powder before serving.

Fabienne Viner-Luzzato
Boulou

A Jewish Tunisian tradition to throw into the mix! These boulou, which are a cross between a cake and a biscuit, are usually served at the end of Yom Kippur with a black coffee. You dip the slice of boulou in the coffee; they half melt and then finish melting in your mouth!

Makes: 3 boulou (each one will cut into several slices; number of slices depends on thickness)
Prep time: 30 minutes • **Cook time:** 15–20 minutes

2 large eggs
150g/5½oz/¾ cup caster
   or granulated sugar
2 tsp vanilla sugar
125ml/4fl oz/½ cup
   vegetable or sunflower
   oil
about 500g/1lb 2oz/
   3¾ cups self-raising
   flour, plus (optional)
   extra for dusting
100g/3½oz/⅔ cup dark
   chocolate chips
50g/1¾oz/⅓ cup raisins
50g/1¾oz/⅓ cup flaked
   almonds

1. Preheat the oven to 200°C/180°C fan/400°F/Gas Mark 6. Line a baking sheet with non-stick baking paper.

2. Place the eggs, both sugars and the vegetable or sunflower oil in a mixing bowl and mix together using a fork. Start adding the flour slowly, mixing with your hands to form a dough. Mix the flour in well, avoiding leaving behind lumps of flour. Add enough flour to make a soft dough – the consistency of the dough needs to be soft, easy to touch but still slightly sticky.

3. On the work surface, divide your dough into three equal portions to make three different flavoured boulou. Add the chocolate chips to one portion of dough, the raisins to another and the flaked almonds to the final portion of dough, kneading each flavouring into the dough until evenly distributed.

4. Roll the flavoured portions of dough into three equal-length logs (you might need to dust the work surface with a little flour first) and then flatten each one into a rectangle about 5cm/2in wide and 15–20cm/6–8in long, then place on the lined baking sheet.

5. Bake for 15–20 minutes, until they become golden brown. Remove from the oven and transfer to a wire rack, then leave to cool completely. Once cool, cut into 2cm/¾in-thick slices to serve (or you can cut them into thinner slices, if you prefer).

6. Store the baked logs in an airtight container at room temperature for up to 4–5 days, and slice them fresh, as needed. They will keep for longer, but will dry a little – but they will still taste amazing dipped in hot black coffee!

Cook's Tip
• If you prefer, you can mix all the flavouring ingredients together (the chocolate chips, raisins and almonds), then simply divide this mixture into three and knead one portion into each portion of dough.

Jessie and Lennie Ware
'Triple Threat' Chocolate Brownies

Jessie recalls that people have requested this recipe the most after hearing about it in the Ed Sheeran [Table Manners podcast] episode. A triple shot of chocolatey goodness, my doctor brother Alex says that it's more like a 'triple threat' to your cholesterol levels, but don't let that stop you from making them.

Get creative! Add whatever you like to your brownie batter. Generous chunks of white, milk or dark chocolate will all work well, as will roughly broken-up Oreos or any other chocolate confectionery. I generally add three things to mine, hence the triple threat. Experiment. Ultimately, whatever you choose will be delicious.

Makes: 9–18 brownies • **Prep time:** 25 minutes • **Cook time:** 40 minutes

200g/7oz/generous ¾ cup (1¾ sticks) unsalted butter, cubed

200g/7oz/scant 1¼ cups dark chocolate, broken into pieces

3 large eggs

275g/9¾oz/scant 1½ cups caster or granulated sugar

90g/3¼oz/⅔ cup plain flour

50g/1¾oz/½ cup unsweetened cocoa powder

250–300g/9–10½oz ingredients of your choice to add to the mix (white, dark or milk chocolate, chocolate biscuits, your favourite chocolate bar), chopped

1. Preheat the oven to 190°C/170°C fan/375°F/Gas Mark 5. Line a 23cm/9in square baking tin with non-stick baking paper.

2. Put the butter and chocolate into a heatproof bowl set over a pan of barely simmering water (ensuring the bottom of the bowl doesn't touch the water underneath). Leave until they start to melt, then stir regularly until fully melted and combined. Remove from the heat and leave to cool a little.

3. In a large bowl, using an electric handheld mixer or stand mixer, whisk the eggs and sugar together on high speed until pale and almost doubled in volume. Add the cooled chocolate and butter mix and gently combine, using a spatula and figure-of-eight motion to fold the two mixtures into one another.

4. Sift the flour and cocoa powder together and then fold into the chocolate and egg mixture. Again, fold gently using a figure-of-eight motion until all is combined. It will appear dusty at first, but be patient and it will come together. Take care not to overdo the mixing: as soon as you cannot see any dusty flour mix, you are there.

5. Now add your extra ingredients and fold in, reserving a few to scatter over the top. Transfer the mixture to the baking tin, levelling it out and pressing any reserved ingredients into the top of the mixture.

6. Bake for around 35 minutes. The top should be just firm, but the middle should be slightly undercooked and gooey: it will continue to cook in the tin once removed from the oven.

7. Remove from the oven, place on a wire rack and leave the baked brownie to cool completely in the tin before cutting into squares and removing.

8. Store any leftover brownies in an airtight container at room temperature.

David Lebovitz
Robert's Absolute Best Brownies

I have a blanket mistrust of any recipe with a superlative in the title. 'The ultimate' or 'The world's finest' always makes me raise an eyebrow. But how else can I describe these brownies? I've made a lot of brownies in my life, and these really are the best. I learned to make them from the late Robert Steinberg, who changed the world of American chocolate when he co-founded Scharffen Berger chocolate. Part of Robert's unique charm was that he was quick to argue, but I learned that like most people who hold strong opinions (at least food-wise), they're invariably right when you taste the results. He adapted his recipe from one by cookbook author Maida Heatter.

The first time I made these brownies, they were a dry, crumbly disaster. Still unconvinced that they were worthy of their accolades, I listened carefully as he walked me through the steps. When he asked if I had stirred the batter vigorously for 1 full minute, I stammered and then finally admitted that I cut that step short. "Aha!" he said. So I made them again, and discovered that that was one life-changing minute.

Makes: 9–12 brownies (or more, depending on how big you like them!)
Prep time: 25 minutes • **Cook time:** 35 minutes

85g/3oz/generous ⅓ cup (¾ stick) unsalted or salted butter, cut into pieces, plus extra for greasing (or use non-stick cooking spray for greasing)

225g/8oz/1⅓ cups dark chocolate (at least 45% cocoa solids), chopped

1 tsp vanilla extract

150g/5½oz/¾ cup caster or granulated sugar

2 large eggs, at room temperature

35g/1¼oz/¼ cup plain flour

135g/4¾oz/1⅓ cups walnuts, almonds, hazelnuts or pecans, toasted and coarsely chopped

1. Preheat the oven to 180°C/160°C fan/350°F/Gas Mark 4. Line the inside of a 23cm/9in square cake tin with two lengths of foil, positioning the sheets perpendicular to each other and allowing the excess to extend beyond the edges of the tin. Or, use one large sheet of extra-wide foil or non-stick baking paper. Lightly grease the foil or paper with butter or non-stick cooking spray.

2. In a medium saucepan, melt the butter, then add the chocolate and stir over a low heat until the chocolate is melted and smooth. Remove from the heat and stir in the vanilla and sugar until combined. Beat in the eggs, one at a time. Add the flour and stir energetically for 1 full minute (don't skip this bit!), until the batter loses its graininess, becomes smooth, and pulls away a bit from the sides of the saucepan. Stir in the chopped nuts.

3. Scrape the batter into the prepared tin, levelling it out, then bake until the centre feels almost set, about 30 minutes. Don't overbake.

4. Remove from the oven and leave to cool completely in the tin before lifting out the foil or baking paper to remove the brownies. Cut into squares or rectangles to serve.

5. These brownies will keep well in an airtight container at room temperature for up to 4 days and can be frozen for up to 1 month.

Variation

This recipe takes well to mix-ins. I'll sometimes add 45g/1¾oz/ ⅓ cup chopped dried cherries or 45g/1¾oz ⅓ cup raw cacao nibs to the batter.

To make Minty Brownies, crush 50g/1¾oz peppermint sweets in a sturdy food bag. Add the crushed mints to the brownies along with the nuts (or omit the nuts). If you like very minty brownies, add ½ teaspoon of peppermint extract along with the mints.

Chef's Tip

• To cut the brownies perfectly, remove them from the tin, peel away the foil or baking paper and set them on a chopping board. Use a long, serrated bread knife, dipping the blade in very hot water and wiping it on a piece of kitchen paper (paper towel) between cutting each slice. Trim off the edges of the brownies with long, slicing strokes, then use the same motion to cut the brownies into squares or rectangles. For positively picture-perfect brownies with neat, clean edges, freeze the brownies in the tin before removing and cutting (then defrost before serving).

Paula Shoyer
Chocolate Cabernet Mandelbread

Some type of mandelbread, basically Jewish biscotti, can always be found in my freezer in case anyone shows up to visit and needs a cookie with their coffee. This recipe, made with red wine both inside the cookie and on top, is a decidedly adult version of the classic.

Makes: about 30 cookies • **Prep time:** 30 minutes, plus 15 minutes resting • **Cook time:** 35–45 minutes

For the cookies
270g/9¾oz/2 cups plain flour
100g/3½oz/1 cup good-quality (100%) unsweetened cocoa powder
300g/10½oz/1½ cups granulated sugar
2 tsp baking powder
a pinch of salt
60ml/4 tbsp/¼ cup Cabernet red wine
3 large eggs, beaten
150ml/5fl oz/⅔ cup rapeseed or sunflower oil
1 tsp vanilla extract
240g/8¾oz/1½ cups chocolate chips (of your choice)

For the cabernet glaze
140g/5oz/1 cup icing sugar
4–6 tsp Cabernet red wine

Cook's Tip
• I recommend using dark cocoa, sometimes called Dutch-processed.

1. Preheat the oven to 180°C/160°C fan/350°F/Gas Mark 4. Line a large baking sheet with non-stick baking paper.

2. Make the cookies. In a large bowl, mix together the flour, cocoa powder, sugar, baking powder and salt. Add the red wine, eggs, rapeseed or sunflower oil and vanilla and mix the ingredients together until combined. Add the chocolate chips and mix again to evenly distribute the chips. I like to knead them in with my hands to best distribute them.

3. Divide the dough in half and shape each half into a log shape, about 25–30cm/10–12in long, then place on the prepared baking sheet at least 7.5cm/3in apart. Flatten each log/loaf slightly.

4. Bake for 30–35 minutes or until the loaves feel pretty solid on top. Remove from the oven and leave to cool on the baking sheet for 15 minutes. Slide the paper and loaves onto a chopping board. Slice each loaf widthways into 1–2cm/½–¾in-thick slices.

5. Place a new piece of non-stick baking paper on the baking sheet and arrange the sliced cookies on the paper, flat/cut-side down. Return to the oven and bake for a further 5 minutes for cookies that are a bit soft, or bake for a further 7–10 minutes for crispier cookies. Slide the paper off the baking sheet onto a wire rack and leave the cookies to cool completely.

6. To make the glaze, place the icing sugar in a bowl and add 4 teaspoons of the red wine. Whisk well. Add more wine, a teaspoon at a time, until you have a thick glaze that you can drizzle. Drizzle the glaze over the cookies, then leave to dry and harden a little before serving.

7. Store the cookies in an airtight container at room temperature for up to 5 days, or freeze in freezer bags for up to 3 months (defrost before serving).

Kim Kushner
Tahini Chocolate Chunk Cookies with Sea Salt

My kids adore these cookies! They are a combination of three favourite flavours: chocolate, saltiness and earthiness. These cookies are heavenly! The idea of combining the tahini with just a touch of miso came from a friend of mine, Shushy Turin. I added a mix of milk and dark chocolate chunks into a simple, buttery cookie batter and the result is indescribable. You really have to taste them for yourself.

Makes: about 16 cookies • **Prep time:** 25 minutes, plus 10 minutes chilling • **Cook time:** 15 minutes

115g/4oz/½ cup (1 stick) unsalted butter, softened

120ml/4fl oz/½ cup raw (organic) tahini

1 tbsp white miso paste

200g/7oz/1 cup granulated or light soft brown sugar

2 large eggs

1 tsp vanilla extract

130g/4½oz/1 cup plain flour

½ tsp bicarbonate of soda

½ tsp baking powder

1 x 100g/3½oz chocolate bar, chopped into chunks (I use a combination of milk and dark chocolate)

1 tsp sea salt flakes

1. Preheat the oven to 160°C/140°C fan/325°F/Gas Mark 3. Line two baking sheets with non-stick baking paper.

2. In an electric stand mixer fitted with the paddle attachment, combine the butter, tahini, miso and sugar. Beat together on a high speed until creamy, about 2 minutes. Add the eggs, one at a time, beating each until incorporated, then add the vanilla.

3. Add the flour, bicarbonate of soda and baking powder and mix on a low speed until combined. Stir in the chocolate chunks. Transfer the mixture to the fridge and chill for at least 10 minutes to firm it up a little (you can refrigerate it for longer, but remember that the longer it is chilled for, the longer the cookies may take to cook).

4. Use a small ice-cream scoop or a tablespoon to scoop the mixture into mounds on the prepared baking sheets, making sure you place them about 7.5cm/3in apart. Sprinkle the tops with a pinch of sea salt flakes.

5. Bake until the edges are browned and the centres are firm, about 15 minutes.

6. Remove from the oven and leave the cookies to cool slightly on the baking sheets, then transfer them to a wire rack and leave to cool completely before serving. Store in an airtight container.

Cook's Tips
• If you don't have a stand mixer, you can make the cookie mixture by hand using a wooden spoon in a bowl.
• These cookies can be stored in an airtight container at room temperature for up to 4 days. I suggest placing non-stick baking paper squares between each cookie to prevent sticking.
• They can also be stored in an airtight container in the freezer for up to 2 months. Again, I suggest placing paper between each cookie. Defrost at room temperature for about 20 minutes before serving.

Gil Hovav
Magic Squares

I know only two kitchen rules… Everything tastes better if you deep-fry it (including my glasses). Nutella makes anything better. Even herring.

So, these magic squares, rich with chocolate, Nutella, ganache, cereals and cocoa – this is the stuff dreams are made of.

Makes: 20–30 squares • **Prep time:** 30 minutes, plus freezing • **Cook time:** 5 minutes

For the base mixture
50g/1¾oz/scant ¼ cup butter
200g/7oz plain butter biscuits, such as petit beurre
50g/1¾oz/2 cups breakfast cereal, such as cornflakes
50g/1¾oz/scant ⅓ cup bittersweet or dark chocolate (preferably 60% cocoa solids), broken into pieces
1 tsp vanilla extract
250g/9oz/1 cup Nutella

For the ganache
250ml/9fl oz/generous 1 cup double cream
300g/10½oz/1¾ cups bittersweet or dark chocolate, broken into pieces
1 tsp vanilla extract

2–3 tbsp unsweetened cocoa powder, for dusting

1. For the base mixture, gently melt the butter in a small pan. Meanwhile, crush together the biscuits and cereal to rough crumbs, either by pulsing in a food processor or by placing them in a freezer bag and bashing with a rolling pin.

2. Take the melted butter off the heat, add the chocolate pieces and vanilla (but don't stir) and wait for 3–4 minutes, then stir until the chocolate has melted. Add the Nutella and crushed biscuits/cereal mixture and mix again until combined.

3. Transfer to a shallow 20 x 30cm/8 x 12in baking/cake tin and flatten evenly. Set aside.

4. Prepare the ganache. Put the cream into a small pan and heat gently until it simmers, then add the chocolate and vanilla, but don't stir. Remove the pan from the heat and wait for 3–4 minutes, then stir until the chocolate has melted and the mixture is smooth and combined.

5. Pour into the tin over the base mixture and spread to cover it completely. Transfer to the freezer and freeze for at least 4 hours.

6. Remove the mixture from the tin in a slab, transferring it onto a chopping (cutting) board. Dust the top with sifted cocoa powder and then cut into little magic squares to serve. Serve immediately (frozen) or keep in an airtight container in the fridge and serve chilled.

7. These magic squares will keep in an airtight container in the fridge for at least 2 weeks (if they last that long!).

Cook's Tip
• If you don't have petit beurre biscuits, shortbread biscuits or digestives (Graham crackers) will also work well.

Jenn Segal
Chocolate Rugelach

A much-loved Jewish holiday treat, rugelach (pronounced rug-a-lah) are miniature pastries posing as cookies. They're made by rolling a buttery, flaky dough around a sweet filling of fruit, nuts, chocolate, or pretty much anything your heart desires. Yiddish for 'little twists', rugelach can be crescent-shaped, or rolled into logs, much like a strudel, and cut into slices before baking.

While they look like fancy bakery cookies, they are totally doable at home. The key is to think ahead: the dough needs to be refrigerated for at least an hour before rolling, and then quickly chilled again before slicing and baking. The unbaked, sliced rugelach can also be chilled and stored in the fridge for up to three days before baking.

Makes: about 36 cookies • **Prep time:** 35 minutes, plus chilling • **Cook time:** 25 minutes

For the dough
340g/11¾oz/2½ cups plain flour, plus extra for dusting
75g/2¾oz/6 tbsp caster or granulated sugar
generous ¼ tsp salt
225g/8oz/1 cup (2 sticks) cold unsalted butter, cut into 2.5cm/1in chunks
175g/6oz/¾ cup cold cream cheese, cut into 2.5cm/1in chunks
1 medium egg yolk

For the filling
225g/8oz/1⅓ cups best-quality semi-sweet or dark chocolate (such as Ghiradelli), roughly chopped
100g/3½oz/½ cup caster or granulated sugar
¼ tsp salt

1. Make the dough. Place the flour, sugar and salt in the bowl of a food processor and pulse a few times to combine. Add the chunks of butter and cream cheese and the egg yolk. Process until the dough starts to come together into a well-moistened, crumbly mass, about 20–30 seconds.

2. Transfer the dough to a clean work surface. Gather the crumbly dough into a ball and knead, dusting the work surface and dough lightly with flour as necessary, until it comes together into a smooth ball.

3. Shape the dough into a rectangle, then cut into 4 equal portions; flatten each piece of dough into a 1cm/½in-thick rectangle. Wrap each portion of dough in clingfilm and refrigerate for at least 1 hour or for up to 3 days.

4. Line a large baking sheet with non-stick baking paper.

5. Make the filling. Place the chocolate in a medium microwave-safe bowl. Melt in the microwave on medium in 30-second bursts, stirring after each burst, until almost melted. Stir, allowing the residual heat in the bowl to melt the chocolate completely. Alternatively, melt the chocolate in a heatproof bowl set over a pan of gently simmering water (ensuring the bottom of the bowl doesn't touch the water underneath). Stir in the sugar and salt – the mixture will be grainy; that's okay.

6. Remove one portion of dough from the fridge, unwrap it and place it on a lightly floured work surface. (If necessary, let it sit at room temperature for a few minutes until it's pliable enough to roll.) Lightly dust the top of the dough with flour, then use a rolling pin to roll it into a 20 x 28cm/8 x 11in rectangle. Don't make yourself crazy over it, but try to make it as even as possible around the edges; it will make it easier to roll. (Trim slightly with a pizza cutter or sharp knife if it's very uneven.)

7. Using a spatula or the back of a spoon, quickly spread a quarter of the chocolate filling evenly over the dough, leaving a 0.5cm/¼in border around the edges. Starting from the long side, roll the dough tightly into a cylinder. Place the filled rolled dough, seam-side down, on the prepared baking sheet.

8. Repeat with the remaining portions of dough and chocolate filling. Place the rolled dough logs in the fridge for 20–30 minutes or until firm to the touch.

9. Preheat the oven to 190°C/170°C fan/375°F/Gas Mark 5.

10. Take the rolled dough out of the fridge. Using a serrated knife, slice off the uneven ends of each roll and discard. Then slice the rolls into 2.5cm/1in-thick pieces. Place each slice, seam-side down, back on the lined baking sheet. Bake for 18–20 minutes or until lightly golden.

11. Remove from the oven and cool the rugelach on the baking sheet for a few minutes, then transfer to a wire rack to cool completely.

12. Rugelach are best enjoyed fresh on the day they are baked, but any leftover cookies can be stored in an airtight container at room temperature for up to 3 days, or frozen for longer storage.

Cook's Tips
- The unbaked sliced rugelach can be frozen for up to 3 months. Before freezing, let the sliced rugelach set on a baking sheet in the freezer for approximately 20 minutes, then transfer to a sealable freezer bag and press out as much air as possible. Bake directly from the freezer, allowing 1–2 minutes longer in the oven.
- To freeze after baking: Let the rugelach cool completely, then store in an airtight container, separating layers with non-stick baking paper or foil. Before serving, remove the cookies from the container and let them come to room temperature.

Amy Lanza
Divine Chocolate Raspberry Caramel Slices

Triple-layered chocolate raspberry caramel slices with an oat and almond biscuit base, a rich and sticky date caramel and mashed fresh raspberries, enrobed in lots of Divine Dark Raspberry Chocolate. These slices make an impressive vegan, gluten-free dessert for friends and family with no baking required.

Makes: 10 squares or bars • **Prep time:** 30 minutes, plus setting/freezing • **Cook time:** 5 minutes

For the base
70g/2½oz/¾ cup rolled
   (old-fashioned) oats or
   oat flour
60g/2¼oz/generous ½ cup
   ground almonds
1 tbsp maple syrup
15g/½oz coconut oil,
   melted

For the caramel
180g/6¼oz/1⅓ cups
   stoned (pitted) dates
a pinch of salt
50g/1¾oz/3½ tbsp nut
   butter of your choice,
   such as almond or
   cashew butter
1 tbsp coconut oil, melted
1 tbsp date water (reserved
   from soaking dates – see
   method) (optional)
125g/4½oz/1 cup fresh
   raspberries, mashed
   with a fork

For the chocolate
120g/4¼oz/¾ cup Divine
   Dark Raspberry
   Chocolate, broken into
   pieces
1 tbsp coconut oil

freeze-dried raspberries, to
   decorate (optional)

1. Line a 20 x 10cm/8 x 4in dish or cake tin with non-stick baking paper. Line a large plate with non-stick baking paper.

2. For the base, if you are starting with oats, add them to a blender and whizz until you have a fine crumble. Now add in all the other base ingredients and pulse to combine. Pour into the lined dish/tin and press down firmly to form an even base layer. Pop in the fridge.

3. Soak the dates in boiling water for 10 minutes and then drain, reserving 1 tablespoon of the soaking liquid. Add the dates to a clean blender with the salt, nut butter and coconut oil and blend until thick and jammy. If needed, add the reserved (1 tablespoon) date soaking water to help it blend.

4. Spread the caramel layer over the base and then top with the mashed raspberries in an even layer. Place in the freezer for 2 hours to set.

5. Remove from the freezer and leave to rest for 15 minutes. Meanwhile, for the chocolate layer, melt the chocolate pieces and coconut oil in a heatproof bowl. Set over a pan of gently simmering water, ensuring the bottom of the bowl doesn't touch the water, and leave to melt, then stir to combine.

6. Remove the caramel/raspberry-topped base from the dish/tin and place on a fresh sheet of non-stick baking paper, caramel/raspberry-side up. Cut into 10 squares or bars, then pour over the melted chocolate to coat the pieces. Decorate with freeze-dried raspberries, if you like. Transfer to the lined plate and leave to set in the freezer for 10–15 minutes before serving. These are best stored in the fridge or freezer, but remove and allow them to come to room temperature before eating (about 15–30 minutes).

7. These slices will keep in an airtight container in the fridge for up to 3–5 days, or in the freezer for up to 1 month.

Cook's Tip
• If you prefer a nut-free option, tahini works well in place of nut butter.

Cakes, Loaves & Tarts

Amy Kritzer Becker
Flourless Chocolate Cupcakes with Raspberry Frosting

Why go the whole week of Passover without chocolate cupcakes? These are rich and fudgy topped with a tart (pink!) raspberry frosting. Easy to make and delicious enough to enjoy long after the festival is over.

Makes: 12 cupcakes • **Prep time:** 30 minutes • **Cook time:** 25 minutes

For the cupcakes
115g/4oz/⅔ cup good-
   quality bittersweet or
   dark chocolate, roughly
   chopped
115g/4oz/½ cup (1 stick)
   unsalted butter
150g/5½oz/¾ cup
   granulated sugar
3 large eggs
1½ tsp vanilla extract
⅛ tsp salt
50g/1¾oz/½ cup
   unsweetened cocoa
   powder, sifted

For the raspberry frosting
115g/4oz/½ cup (1 stick)
   unsalted butter, at room
   temperature
275g/9¾oz/2 cups kosher
   for Passover icing sugar,
   sifted
1 tsp vanilla extract
65g/2½oz/½ cup fresh
   raspberries, rinsed and
   dried well, plus 12 extra
   (optional) to decorate
a splash of whole milk or
   water (optional)

1. Preheat the oven to 180°C/160°C fan/350°F/Gas Mark 4. Line a 12-hole cupcake tin with paper cases and set aside.

2. First up, for the cupcakes, melt your chocolate and butter in a medium saucepan over a low heat, stirring, until smooth. (I used bittersweet chocolate but dark chocolate would be awesome, too!) Measure out the granulated sugar into a large, heatproof bowl and set aside.

3. Add the warm chocolate mixture to the sugar and beat with an electric handheld mixer just until incorporated (or beat together by hand using a wooden spoon). Leave to cool.

4. Add the eggs to the chocolate mixture, one at a time, beating after each addition. Stir in the vanilla, the salt and cocoa powder, mixing until combined.

5. Spoon the mixture into the cupcake cases, dividing it evenly. Bake for 20 minutes or until a cocktail stick inserted in the middle comes out clean. Remove from the oven and cool in the tin for 5 minutes, then transfer the cupcakes to a wire rack and leave to cool completely.

6. While your cupcakes are baking, let's make the frosting! Beat the softened butter, icing sugar and vanilla together in a bowl with an electric handheld mixer until smooth and combined (or you can do this by hand using a wooden spoon, but it will take more effort to get it as smooth).

7. Next up, add in the raspberries and beat until smooth. If the frosting is a little dry, add a splash of milk or cold water to the mix. If it is too runny, add more icing sugar. It should be thick but spreadable. That's it!

8. Pipe or spread the frosting onto your cooled cupcakes and top each one with a raspberry, if desired (I desired!). These cupcakes are super rich and gooey.

9. Once frosted, these cupcakes are best eaten on the same day. The unfrosted cupcakes will keep in an airtight container at room temperature for up to 2 days.

Martyne Burman
Chocolate Beetroot Cake

I have a fantastically sweet tooth! So, in an effort to make a sin into a virtue, I started experimenting with putting vegetables into cakes and this delicious chocolate beetroot cake is one of them. It tastes truly indulgent and it's a good way to get another vegetable into your children.

Serves: 6–8 (depending on your appetite!) • **Prep time:** 25 minutes • **Cook time:** 25–45 minutes

145g/5¼oz/generous 1 cup plain flour
65g/2½oz/⅔ cup good-quality unsweetened cocoa powder
1½ tsp baking powder
200g/7oz/1 cup caster or granulated sugar
200g/7oz/1½ cups cooked, peeled beetroots/beets (not in vinegar), finely grated (shredded)
2 large eggs, beaten
1 tsp vanilla essence
160ml/5½fl oz/⅔ cup sunflower oil

1. Preheat the oven to 180°C/160°C fan/350°F/Gas Mark 4. Either line an 8-hole muffin tin with paper cases, or grease and line a deep 20cm/8in round cake tin with non-stick baking paper.

2. Sift the flour, cocoa powder and baking powder into a mixing bowl, then stir in the sugar. Set aside.

3. In a separate bowl, mix together the grated beetroot, eggs and vanilla essence with a wooden spoon, then add the sunflower oil and mix until smooth.

4. Make a well in the centre of the dry ingredients and add the egg mixture, then lightly mix together until combined.

5. Either spoon the mixture into the muffin cases, dividing it evenly, or transfer the mixture to the prepared cake tin, spreading it level.

6. Bake the muffins for 25 minutes or until the tops are firm and bounce back when pressed lightly with your finger. Alternatively, bake the cake for about 45 minutes or until a skewer inserted into the centre comes out with a little mixture still sticking to it, as it's a very moist cake.

7. Remove from the oven and cool for a couple of minutes in the muffin or cake tin, then transfer the muffins to, or turn the cake out onto, a wire rack and leave to cool. Serve warm or cold.

8. Store in an airtight container at room temperature for up a week (though I doubt it will last that long!).

Cook's Tips
• Once cooled, you can dust the muffins or cake with a little icing sugar to decorate, if you like. They are also delicious served warm with custard.
• The cold cake can also be cut in half horizontally and then sandwiched together with a chocolate buttercream icing (or the muffins can be topped with chocolate buttercream), but this does make a very rich dessert!

Oren Goldfeld
Chocolate Tart with Mahlab

The smell of mahlab is something I remember from childhood at my maternal grandparents. Usually used in baked goods, I love using it in sweet desserts as well because of its marzipan-like flavour. Try it in crème brûlée instead of vanilla, or in this case with chocolate, for a perfect flavour combination.

Serves: 8 • **Prep time:** 35 minutes, plus chilling and steeping • **Cook time:** 1 hour 20 minutes

For the shortcrust pastry
250g/9oz/scant 2 cups plain flour, plus extra for dusting
85g/3oz/generous ¾ cup unsweetened cocoa powder
190g/6¾oz/scant 1 cup caster or granulated sugar
¼ tsp salt
200g/7oz/generous ¾ cup (1¾ sticks) unsalted butter, cold and cut into cubes
1 large egg
1 tbsp cold water

For the chocolate mahlab filling
1½ tsp ground mahlab
1 single espresso or 40ml/1½fl oz freshly made coffee, warm
300g/10½oz/1¾ cups dark chocolate, broken into pieces
4 large eggs
50g/1¾oz/¼ cup light soft brown sugar
120ml/4fl oz/½ cup double cream

1. For the pastry, place the flour, cocoa powder, sugar and salt in a food processor. Add the cubes of butter and pulse until the mixture resembles breadcrumbs. Add the egg and cold water and pulse until the dough comes together. Tip the dough out onto the work surface and flatten into a disc, then wrap in clingfilm and chill in the fridge for 30 minutes.

2. Preheat the oven to 180°C/160°C fan/350°F/Gas Mark 4.

3. On a floured surface, or between two sheets of non-stick baking paper, roll out the pastry and use it to line a 23cm/9in round tart tin. Trim the edges and prick the base with a fork, then line with ovenproof clingfilm or non-stick baking paper and fill with baking beans. Bake for 20 minutes, then carefully remove the baking beans and clingfilm/paper and bake for a further 5 minutes.

4. Reduce the oven temperature to 150°C/130°C fan/300°F/Gas Mark 2.

5. For the filling, in a cup or small bowl, mix the mahlab with the warm espresso/coffee. Warm it back up to about 60°C/140°F in a microwave or in a pan on the hob and then set aside to steep for 20 minutes.

6. Meanwhile, melt the chocolate in a heatproof bowl set over a pan of gently simmering water, ensuring the bottom of the bowl doesn't touch the water. Stir until smooth, then remove from the heat and allow it to cool slightly.

7. In a bowl of an electric stand mixer, whisk the eggs and brown sugar for about 6 minutes until thick and pale. Fold the whisked egg mixture into the melted chocolate. Strain the coffee from the mahlab grounds (discard the grounds) and gently whisk into the chocolate mixture followed by the double cream until incorporated, then pour into the tart case.

8. Bake for about 50 minutes, until set, but do check it after 30 minutes. Once it's ready, the filling will still have a slight wobble and a cocktail stick inserted into the centre will come out with some crumbs sticking to it.

9. Remove from the oven and leave the tart to cool in the tin to room temperature, then carefully remove and place on a serving plate. The tart can be served at room temperature (or warmed up slightly, if you prefer). Serve the tart on its own or with a dollop of crème fraîche alongside.

10. The baked tart will keep in an airtight container at room temperature for up to 3 days, or in the fridge for up to 5 days.

Chef's Tip
• To make the pastry without a food processor, simply sift the flour and cocoa powder into a bowl, stir in the sugar and salt, then lightly rub in the cubes of butter until the mixture resembles breadcrumbs. Add the egg and cold water and mix to a dough, then shape, wrap and chill as above.

Tester's Tip
• For a final flourish, sprinkle a pinch of sea salt flakes over the top. (JR)

Paola Gavin
Chocolate Hazelnut Cake

This delicious flourless chocolate cake is often served during Passover and for special occasions. It is usually topped with a chocolate icing, but is also very good simply dusted with icing sugar and served with a dollop of whipped cream.

Serves: 8 • **Prep time:** 35 minutes • **Cook time:** 1 hour – 1 hour 5 minutes

butter, for greasing

caster or granulated sugar or potato flour, for dusting

2–3 tbsp chopped blanched hazelnuts or almonds, to decorate (optional)

For the cake

150g/5½oz/generous 1 cup whole blanched hazelnuts

1 tsp baking powder

125g/4½oz/¾ cup dark chocolate (70% cocoa solids), broken into squares

5 medium eggs, separated, plus 1 medium egg

150g/5½oz/¾ cup caster or granulated sugar

For the icing

125g/4½oz/¾ cup dark chocolate (70% cocoa solids), broken into squares

2 tbsp rum or hazelnut liqueur

3½ tsp unsalted butter

1. Preheat the oven to 160°C/140°C fan/325°F/Gas Mark 3. Grease a 23cm/9in round springform cake tin with butter and dust with sugar or potato flour.

2. Place the hazelnuts for the cake on a baking sheet in a single layer and roast for 10–12 minutes or until lightly browned, stirring from time to time so they roast evenly. Remove from the oven and allow to cool slightly.

3. Turn the oven up to 180°C/160°C fan/350°F/Gas Mark 4. Process the toasted nuts in a blender until finely ground. Stir in the baking powder.

4. Melt the chocolate in a heatproof bowl set over a pan of gently simmering water, taking care not to let the bottom of the bowl touch the water. Set aside to cool slightly.

5. In a mixing bowl, beat the egg yolks and whole egg with half of the sugar until light and creamy. Add the melted chocolate and mix well, then fold in the ground hazelnuts.

6. In a separate mixing bowl, whisk the egg whites with the remaining sugar until stiff peaks form, then fold into the chocolate mixture. Pour the batter into the prepared tin.

7. Bake for 40–45 minutes or until a knife inserted into the centre comes out clean. Remove from the oven, unclip the tin and leave the cake to cool for 2–3 minutes, then turn out onto a wire rack and leave it to cool completely.

8. To make the icing, melt the chocolate in a heatproof bowl set over a pan of gently simmering water. Stir in the rum or hazelnut liqueur, then remove from the heat and beat in the butter, a little at a time, until the icing is smooth and creamy.

9. Set the icing aside for about 5 minutes, until it is cool but not set, then spread over the top of the cake.

10. Store leftovers in an airtight container at room temperature for up to 3 days.

Lisa Goldberg & The Monday Morning Cooking Club
Chocolate and Marmalade Celebration Cake

This chocolate cake was first published in our book (*Monday Morning Cooking Club – the food, the stories, the sisterhood*). It came from Sydney matriarch and great-grandmother, Elza Levin, and may just be the most frequently baked cake in our collection. It is a make-it-with-your-eyes-closed, you've-got-everything-in-your-pantry kind of cake. For this oversized celebration of double chocolate goodness, which is in our most recent book (*Now for Something Sweet*), you will need to make two cakes (the recipe has the quantities and recipe for one) and we have added our touch with a homemade marmalade and buttercream icing.

Serves: about 20 • **Prep time:** 50 minutes (for the cake) • **Cook time:** 3 hours 10 minutes

For each cake
(you need to make two)

250g/9oz/generous 1 cup (2¼ sticks) unsalted butter, chopped, plus extra for greasing

200g/7oz/scant 1¼ cups best-quality dark chocolate, roughly chopped

1 tbsp instant coffee granules

375ml/13fl oz/1⅔ cups hot water (from just-boiled kettle or hot tap)

460g/1lb ½oz/2¼ cups caster or granulated sugar

185g/6½oz/1⅓ cups self-raising flour

75g/2¾oz/generous ½ cup plain flour

30g/1oz/¼ cup best-quality unsweetened cocoa powder

2 large eggs

2 tsp vanilla extract

1. You need to make two cakes for this double chocolate marmalade cake.

2. To make one cake, preheat the oven to 150°C/130°C fan/300°F/Gas Mark 2. Grease and line the base and sides of a 24cm/9½in round springform cake tin. It is a very liquid batter, so if your tin leaks, secure a piece of foil around the outside of the base and side.

3. Melt the butter in a saucepan over a medium heat and add the chocolate, stirring to melt. Add the coffee, hot water and sugar, stirring until you have a smooth mixture. Remove from the heat and pour into a large, heatproof mixing bowl. Cool for 5 minutes.

4. Sift the flours and the cocoa powder into the chocolate mixture and stir through. Lightly whisk the eggs with the vanilla, then add them to the bowl, beating well by hand or with an electric handheld mixer until you have a smooth batter.

5. Pour the batter into the prepared tin and bake for 1½ hours or until a skewer inserted into the centre comes out clean. The top will be crusty and cracked. If you prefer a smoother top, cut a piece of non-stick baking paper the same size as the cake and place it on top of the mixture during baking.

6. Remove from the oven, place on a wire rack and allow the cake to cool completely before removing it from the tin. Repeat and make a second cake.

7. To make the buttercream icing, beat the butter in a bowl using an electric handheld mixer (or by hand using a wooden spoon) until pale and thick. Sift the icing sugar and cocoa powder together and add to the butter, beating at low speed until combined. Add the milk, vanilla and salt and beat well until you have a smooth icing.

For the buttercream icing
250g/9oz/generous 1 cup
    (2¼ sticks) unsalted
    butter, at room
    temperature, chopped
400g/14oz/2¾ cups icing
    sugar
60g/2¼oz/generous ½ cup
    best-quality
    unsweetened cocoa
    powder
80ml/2¾fl oz/⅓ cup whole
    milk
2 tsp vanilla extract
½ tsp salt

To assemble and finish
200g/7oz/generous ½ cup
    orange marmalade (see
    below and Cook's Tips)
pieces of orange rind from
    the marmalade (see
    below and Cook's Tips)
    or fresh flowers

For the marmalade (makes
    about 500ml/18fl oz/
    generous 2 cups)
4 oranges
1.5 litres/2¾ pints/6 cups
    plus 4 tbsp water
660g/1lb 7½oz/3⅓ cups
    granulated sugar
1 tbsp brandy

8. To assemble the cake, halve each cake horizontally so you end up with two round layers from each (four layers in total). Lay one layer of cake on a serving plate, spread one-third of the marmalade all over it, then a quarter of the buttercream, then top with the next layer of cake and repeat. Top the last layer of cake just with buttercream.

9. Decorate the top with pieces of orange rind from the marmalade or fresh flowers, as you wish.

10. The un-iced cake will keep in an airtight container at room temperature for up to 3 days. The iced cake is best eaten on the day it's made, but can be refrigerated in an airtight container for up to 3 days (allow it to return to room temperature before serving).

For the marmalade

1. Halve and thinly slice the oranges, remove any seeds, then place in a medium, heavy-based saucepan. Add the water and bring to the boil, then reduce the heat and simmer, uncovered, for 1 hour or until the fruit is soft.

2. Stir in the sugar, then simmer for at least 1 hour until a rich syrup forms. The syrup should reduce to about 500ml/18fl oz/generous 2 cups. Once it has reduced, add the brandy and stir.

3. Strain through a colander or sieve to separate the peel from the fruity syrup, as you will need the peel for decoration. You may need to remove any orange flesh still attached to the peel and put it back in with the fruity syrup.

4. Pour the fruity syrup into a clean, warm jam jar, cover and leave to cool and set into marmalade. Set the orange peel aside to cool. You will need all the peel but only half the marmalade for this recipe.

Cook's Tips
• If you don't have time to make the marmalade, you can use store-bought orange marmalade and decorate the cake with candied or glacé orange pieces instead.
• The leftover marmalade will keep in the fridge for up to 3 months.

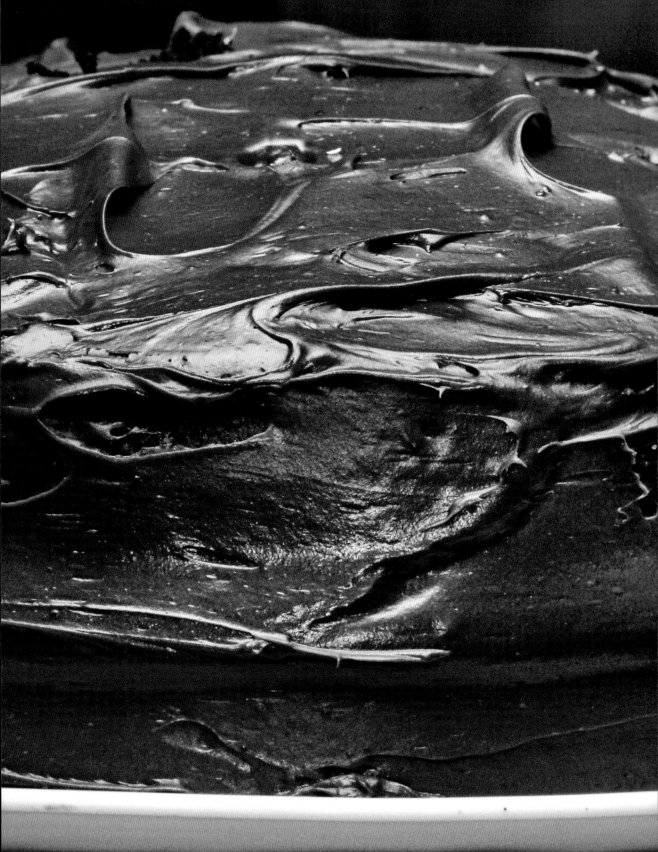

Emma Spitzer
Israeli White Chocolate Cheesecake

I make this cheesecake a lot; it has no boundaries on the sense of occasion it applies to. I make catering size trays of it for parties and it never fails to receive a chorus of praise. It's a no-bake cheesecake, which means there is little that can go wrong, just ensure that you use good-quality cream cheese and don't substitute the biscuits, they are the key ingredient. This needs no accompaniment other than some nice fresh raspberries to cut through the sweetness. It's rich and velvety and incredibly moreish – eat with caution.

Serves: 6–8 • **Prep time:** 30 minutes, plus freezing and chilling • **Cook time:** 5 minutes

For the biscuit base
200g/7oz petit beurre
  biscuits
120g/4¼oz/½ cup plus
  1 tsp (1 stick, plus 1 tsp)
  unsalted butter, melted

For the filling
150g/5½oz/scant 1 cup
  white chocolate, broken
  into pieces
200g/7oz/generous ¾ cup
  (1¾ sticks) unsalted
  butter, softened
125g/4½oz/scant ⅔ cup
  caster or granulated
  sugar
1 large egg plus 1 large egg
  yolk
250g/9oz/generous 1 cup
  good-quality cream
  cheese (I recommend
  Philadelphia)
200g/7ox/scant 1 cup full-
  fat crème fraîche

fresh raspberries, to serve
  (optional)

1. For the biscuit base, add the biscuits to a food processor and blitz to crumbs, then mix with the melted butter. Alternatively, place the biscuits in a freezer bag and bash with a rolling pin to make crumbs, then mix with the melted butter in a bowl.

2. Press two-thirds of the mixture into a 20 x 27cm/8 x 10¾in baking dish, flattening it out so that it forms an even layer. Place in the freezer for 15 minutes until it is set.

3. Meanwhile, prepare the filling. Put the chocolate pieces in a heatproof bowl and either set over a saucepan of gently simmering water (ensuring the bottom of the bowl doesn't touch the water underneath) and leave until melted, or heat in the microwave on medium in 30-second bursts, until melted, stirring after each burst. Remove the bowl from the pan or microwave and leave to cool slightly.

4. While the chocolate is melting and cooling, beat the softened butter, sugar, whole egg and egg yolk together in an electric stand mixer fitted with the paddle attachment until fluffy (or in a bowl with a wooden spoon and develop some muscle at the same time!); this will take around 10 minutes.

5. Beat the cream cheese and crème fraîche together in a separate bowl, then stir in the melted chocolate. Add to the butter and sugar mixture, then carefully fold all the ingredients together.

6. Spread the mixture evenly over the biscuit base and top with the remaining biscuit crumbs. Leave to set in the fridge for a minimum of 3 hours, but 24 hours is preferable. Serve in slices with some fresh raspberries to accompany, if you like.

7. To store any leftovers, cover the dish with clingfilm and keep in the fridge for up to 3–4 days.

Judy Jackson
Chocolate Mousse Cake

This is a flourless cake (suitable for gluten-free diets). It is pareve and easy to prepare ahead, so it is good for Shabbat and Festival meals. I originally learned to make chocolate mousse from my mother, a maths graduate and meticulous cook, who came from Lisbon. This new version comes from my daughter-in-law in Israel, Karen Miller Jackson, who makes huge and fantastic meals for Shabbat.

Serves: 8 • **Prep time:** 25 minutes • **Cook time:** 35–40 minutes

225g/8oz/1⅓ cups good-quality dark chocolate (60–70% cocoa solids), broken into small pieces

60ml/4 tbsp/¼ cup sunflower oil, plus extra for greasing

1 tsp vanilla extract (or omit this and use vanilla sugar)

8 large eggs, separated

225g/8oz/generous 1 cup caster or granulated sugar

2 tsp grated good-quality dark chocolate, to decorate (optional)

1. Preheat the oven to 180°C/160°C fan/350°F/Gas Mark 4. Grease a 20cm/8in round springform cake tin with a little oil.

2. Place the chocolate pieces, sunflower oil and vanilla in a heatproof bowl set over a pan of gently simmering water, stirring occasionally until the mixture is smooth and combined. Alternatively, you can do this in a microwave on medium in 30-second bursts, until melted and combined, but take care to stop and stir after each burst to ensure it doesn't overcook. Once melted, set aside to cool to lukewarm.

3. Place the egg yolks in a mixing bowl and whisk, then gradually add half the sugar, whisking the yolks and sugar together until they are thick and a pale yellow – this is easiest done using an electric handheld mixer or stand mixer.

4. In a separate clean bowl, whisk the egg whites with the remaining sugar until stiff peaks form. Fold them into the egg yolk mixture, then fold in the melted chocolate until just combined (don't overmix).

5. Spoon three-quarters of mousse mixture into the springform tin, levelling out the top. Cover and refrigerate the remaining mousse mixture.

6. Bake the cake for about 30–35 minutes until it is just set. You can tell if the cake is done by testing it with a cocktail stick (toothpick) or a strand of raw spaghetti. If this comes out clean when inserted into the centre of the cake, then it is done. If not, bake for a few more minutes and test again.

7. Remove the cake from the oven, place on a wire rack and leave it to cool completely in the tin – it will sink in the middle as it cools (this is meant to happen!). Once it is cold, spoon the remaining chilled mousse mixture over the top in an even layer, smoothing it out.

8. To serve, run a palette knife around the edge of the cake, loosen the tin clip, then gently push the cake up from the bottom and transfer to a serving plate. Decorate with the grated chocolate, if you like, then serve.

Cook's Tip
• You can make the cake the day before and keep it in the fridge to finish it the next day. Once baked and cooled, simply refrigerate it in the tin, then add the final layer later just before serving.

Rabbi Deborah R. Prinz
Basque Chocolate Cake

This unique combination of chocolate and cherries directs our taste buds to the flavours of the Basque area of Bayonne, France, where Jews, exiled from Spain, are said to have initiated chocolate-making in France.

Serves: 6–8 • **Prep time:** 25 minutes • **Cook time:** 30–40 minutes

170g/6oz/¾ cup
(1½ sticks) unsalted
butter, diced, plus extra
for greasing
150g/5½oz/scant 1 cup
bittersweet or dark
chocolate (70% cocoa
solids), broken into
pieces
3 large eggs
150g/5½oz/¾ cup
granulated sugar
45g/1¾oz/⅓ cup plain
flour, plus extra for
dusting

To serve
220g/8oz/¾ cup black
cherry jam (preserves)
crème fraîche

1. Preheat the oven to 190°C/170°C fan/375°F/Gas Mark 5. Lightly butter and flour a 23cm/9in round cake tin.

2. Place a large heatproof bowl over a pan of simmering water, ensuring the bottom of the bowl doesn't touch the water. Add the butter and chocolate to the bowl and leave to melt, stirring frequently, until smooth, about 4 minutes. Remove from the heat and leave it to cool slightly.

3. In a medium bowl, using an electric handheld mixer or stand mixer (or using a balloon whisk, by hand), whisk the eggs with the sugar on high speed until thick and pale, about 3 minutes (it will take a bit longer if doing it by hand). Add the flour and whisk on low speed until just combined. Fold in one-third of the melted chocolate mixture, then gently fold in the remaining melted chocolate; do not overmix. Pour the batter into the prepared tin, spreading it level, if needed.

4. Bake for 20–30 minutes or until a cocktail stick (toothpick) inserted into the centre comes out clean. Remove from the oven and leave to cool in the tin for a few minutes, then turn the cake out onto a wire rack and leave to cool completely.

5. When you are ready to serve, warm through the cherry jam in a small pan over a medium heat. Cut the cake into slices and serve some of the cherry jam and a dollop of crème fraîche on top of each slice.

6. Store any leftover cake in an airtight container at room temperature for up to a few days, then serve with the accompaniments, as before.

Cook's Tip
• It can be served on its own, but I recommend serving it with the cherry jam and crème fraîche every time!

Joan Nathan
Chocolate Almond Cake

This recipe for chocolate almond cake is 400 years old, and was passed down orally in one Bayonne family from mother to daughter in Spanish, Ladino and then in French. The accent of rum was probably introduced in the seventeenth century. My guess is that at first the eggs would have been whole, and later separated, the whites whipped to give it more height, probably in the eighteenth century. This cake can be made with matzo cake meal for Passover.

Serves: 8 • **Prep time:** 25 minutes • **Cook time:** 35–40 minutes

For the cake
225g/8oz/1⅓ cups good-quality bittersweet or dark chocolate, roughly chopped
100g/3½oz/scant ½ cup (7 tbsp) unsalted butter or pareve margarine, plus extra for greasing
150g/5½oz/¾ cup granulated sugar
¼ tsp salt
3 large eggs, separated
1 tsp vanilla extract
150g/5½oz/1¼ cups finely chopped blanched almonds
65g/2½oz/½ cup plain flour or matzo cake meal

For the glaze
50g/1¾oz/6 tbsp icing sugar
1 tbsp rum
1 tbsp water

fresh raspberries and whipped cream, to decorate and serve (optional)

1. Preheat the oven to 180°C/160°C fan/350°F/Gas Mark 4. Grease a 23cm/9in round springform cake tin or deep round cake tin.

2. To make the cake, melt the chocolate in a heatproof bowl set over a pan of gently simmering water, ensuring the bottom of the bowl doesn't touch the water. Once melted, remove from the heat and leave it to cool slightly.

3. Using an electric stand mixer fitted with the paddle attachment, cream the butter or margarine, granulated sugar and salt together until light and fluffy (or you can do this by hand in a bowl using a wooden spoon). Mix the cooled, melted chocolate into the creamed mixture, then add the egg yolks, one at a time, beating well after each addition. Finally, mix in the vanilla, almonds and flour or matzo cake meal until combined.

4. In a separate clean bowl, with clean beaters (or using a balloon whisk by hand), whisk the egg whites to stiff peaks. Fold the egg whites into the cake mixture. Pour the cake mixture into the prepared springform cake tin, levelling the surface if necessary.

5. Bake for 30–35 minutes or until risen and cooked – to make sure it is done, insert a skewer or cocktail stick into the centre of the cake; it should come out clean. Remove from the oven to a wire rack and leave to cool completely in the tin. Once cold, remove the cake from the tin.

6. To make the glaze, in a small bowl, dissolve the icing sugar in the rum and water, mixing well. Pour the glaze evenly over the cold cake. Decorate with fresh raspberries (if using), then cut into slices and serve each portion with a dollop of whipped cream, if you like.

7. The glazed (undecorated) cake will keep in an airtight container at room temperature for a few days.

Sarit Packer
Dark and White Chocolate Marble Cake

As children growing up, a version of this cake was a staple of weekend kitchen counter snacking and school bake sales, but our childhood versions never seem to live up to the funky appearance – so we developed a grown-up version which will satisfy everyone.

The white chocolate cake batter is flavoured with vanilla and orange, and the dark chocolate batter is laced with coffee and cinnamon. Both pack a deep flavour punch that will have everyone wanting more.

Makes: 1 loaf cake • **Prep time:** 35 minutes, plus 10 minutes resting • **Cook time:** 1 hour – 1 hour 5 minutes

For the base batter
200g/7oz/generous ¾ cup (1¾ sticks) unsalted butter, at room temperature, plus extra for greasing
380g/13¼oz/scant 2 cups light soft brown sugar
3 medium eggs
350g/12oz/2⅔ cups white spelt flour (or you can use plain)
2 tsp baking powder
½ tsp salt

For the white-chocolate layers
120ml/4fl oz/½ cup whole milk
100g/3½oz/scant ⅔ cup white chocolate, broken into pieces
seeds scraped from 1 vanilla pod
finely grated zest of 1 orange

For the chocolate-and-coffee layers
120ml/4fl oz/½ cup whole milk
100g/3½oz/scant ⅔ cup dark chocolate (50–70%

1. Preheat the oven to 190°C/170°C fan/375°F/Gas Mark 5. Grease and line a large (2kg/4½lb) loaf tin with non-stick baking paper (or you can use a large Bundt tin or a deep 23cm/9in round cake tin).

2. Make the base batter. Using an electric stand mixer fitted with the paddle attachment, cream the butter and brown sugar together until well combined and creamy. Add the eggs, one at a time, mixing between each addition, then mix in the flour, baking powder and salt. Divide the cake batter between two mixing bowls and set aside.

3. To make the chocolate layers, pour both lots of milk (so 240ml/8fl oz/1 cup) into a saucepan and heat gently until boiling. Meanwhile, place the white and dark chocolates each into a separate heatproof bowl with their respective flavourings. Pour half the hot milk (120ml/4fl oz/½ cup) into each bowl over the chocolate and flavourings. Leave to rest for 5 minutes before stirring to combine with the flavourings. Add each bowlful of melted chocolate to a portion of the cake batter and mix well.

4. Layer the two cake batters in the prepared loaf tin, adding a scoopful of one, then a scoopful of the other, and so on, until you have used up all the cake batters – the tin should be about three-quarters full.

5. Bake in the centre of the oven for 30 minutes. Rotate the tin and bake for another 24–30 minutes or until the cake is fully set and bouncy.

6. Remove from the oven and leave to rest in the tin for 10 minutes before turning it out onto a wire rack to cool completely. Cut into slices to serve.

7. This will keep in an airtight container at room temperature for a few days.

cocoa solids – I tend to use 70%), broken into pieces
1 tbsp unsweetened cocoa powder
1 tsp instant coffee powder
1 tsp ground cinnamon

Cook's Tip
● If you don't have a stand mixer, you can make the cake batters by hand, using a wooden spoon and large bowl.

Tester's Tip
● This makes a lot of mixture, so if you don't have a loaf tin large enough, then you can use the leftovers to make another extra cake. (NA)

Rosalind Rathouse
Hazelnut Cake with Chocolate Ganache

Growing up in South Africa and long before carrot cakes were in vogue, my mother 'invented' this wonderfully moist cake. For a rich dessert, I top the cake with a dark chocolate ganache. My mum used a thin rum icing drizzled over the top, which is also delicious and not as rich.

Serves: 12 • **Prep time:** 30 minutes • **Cook time:** 45 minutes

sunflower oil, for greasing

For the cake
5 medium eggs, separated
90g/3¼oz/scant ½ cup caster or granulated sugar
a pinch of salt
250g/9oz/2½ cups ground hazelnuts (finely ground but not to a paste)
1 large carrot (250g/9oz), peeled and finely grated
½ tsp cream of tartar

For the icing
250g/9oz/1½ cups dark chocolate, broken into pieces
250ml/9fl oz/generous 1 cup double cream

1. Preheat the oven to 180°C/160°C fan/350°F/Gas Mark 4. Grease and line the base of a 23cm/9in round springform cake tin. There is no need to grease the sides of the tin.

2. For the cake, put the egg yolks, sugar and salt into a mixing bowl and whisk together until thick and very pale – this is easiest done using an electric stand mixer or handheld mixer as it will take several minutes on high speed. Gently fold in the ground hazelnuts, then fold in the grated carrot.

3. In a separate clean bowl, whisk the egg whites until foamy, then add the cream of tartar and whisk until stiff. Gently fold the whisked egg whites into the egg yolk mixture until combined.

4. Pour the cake mixture into the prepared tin and spread it out, heaping the mixture in the centre a little.

5. Bake for about 40 minutes or until light golden brown and a skewer inserted into the centre of the cake comes out clean. The cake should spring back when touched.

6. Remove from the oven, cool the cake a little in the tin, then release it from the tin, transfer to a wire rack and leave to cool completely before icing.

7. For the icing, place the chocolate pieces in a heatproof bowl and set aside. Pour the cream into a saucepan and heat gently until it reaches scorching point (this is just before boiling point is reached). Pour the hot cream over the chocolate and whisk until fully melted, blended, smooth and shiny. Set the icing aside to cool until it is thick enough to spread.

8. Thickly spread the icing over the top of the cake. Serve in slices.

9. Store any leftovers in an airtight container at room temperature – it should keep for a few days.

Estee Raviv
Tahini Chocolate Chip Banana Bread

I have so many banana bread recipes, but this one is very different to the ones I usually make… Its texture is rich and thick from the tahini, super flavourful and so satisfying. It is high in protein from the tahini and great as a healthy grab-n-go vegan snack/breakfast.

Makes: 1 loaf cake/Serves 10–12 • **Prep time:** 20 minutes • **Cook time:** 30 minutes

olive oil or coconut oil, for
   greasing
3 large bananas, peeled
   and mashed
115g/4oz/½ cup tahini
   (I use Tarazi tahini)
170g/6oz/½ cup pure
   maple syrup
1 tsp vanilla extract
130g/4½oz/1 cup gluten-
   free plain flour blend
1 tsp baking powder
1½ tsp bicarbonate of soda
1 tsp ground cinnamon
pinch of salt
80g/2¾oz/½ cup vegan
   chocolate chips

1. Preheat the oven to 190°C/170°C fan/375°F/Gas Mark 5. Grease a 22 x 13cm/8½ x 5in loaf tin with olive oil or coconut oil.

2. Take a mixing bowl and add the mashed bananas, tahini, maple syrup and vanilla and mix together well.

3. Take another mixing bowl and add the flour, baking powder, bicarbonate of soda, cinnamon, salt and chocolate chips and mix well.

4. Gradually add the dry ingredients to the wet ingredients and mix constantly until well incorporated. Pour the mixture into the prepared loaf tin and level the top, if needed.

5. Bake for about 30 minutes until golden brown. Once it's ready, a cocktail stick inserted into the centre of the cake should come out clean.

6. Remove from the oven, transfer the tin to a wire rack and leave the cake to cool completely in the tin. Once cold, turn the cake out of the tin. Cut into slices to serve – there's no need for accompaniments, as it's super moist and delicious just as it is.

7. The cake will keep in an airtight container in the fridge for up to 5–7 days. To serve, warm up a slice in the microwave.

Nino Shaye Weiss
Sachertorte

Rare are those humans who have never heard of Sachertorte, the world-famous chocolate cake. But few are those who know that its creator was Jewish and why that matters. Franz Sacher was the Jewish pastry chef responsible and, significantly, he was one of a long, abundant line of Central European Jewish pastry professionals. Contrary to popular belief, the cake was not created in 1832 and it was not created in Vienna, but in Pressburg (today's Slovak capital Bratislava).

The 'conching' processes required to produce smooth-melting chocolate needed for the glossy topping of the cake were only available from the second half of the nineteenth century. Sacher himself insisted in an interview given on the occasion of his ninetieth birthday that he first made the Sachertorte around 1850 in Pressburg, where he worked for the nobility at the local casino. You can read the full history on my Jewish Viennese food blog. Here is my version of the cake.

Serves: 12 • **Prep time:** 1 hour, plus chilling • **Cook time:** 55–65 minutes

For the Sacher cake
plain flour, for dusting
80g/2¾oz/½ cup bittersweet or dark chocolate (85% cocoa solids), roughly chopped
85g/3oz/generous ⅓ cup unsalted butter, softened, plus extra for greasing
30g/1oz/3½ tbsp icing sugar
⅛ tsp ground cinnamon
4 large eggs (approx. 57g/2oz each), separated, plus 1 large egg yolk
115g/4oz/generous ½ cup granulated sugar
90g/3¼oz/⅔ cup cake flour or soft cake and pastry flour (in Vienna this is called 'Glatt – Typ 700')

1. One day before serving, preheat the oven to 160°C/140°C fan/325°F/ Gas Mark 3. Butter and flour a 20cm/8in round cake tin that is at least 6cm/2½in deep (or you can butter and line the tin with non-stick baking paper). Line a baking sheet with non-stick baking paper and set aside.

2. For the cake, melt the chocolate in a bain-marie – place the chocolate in a heatproof bowl set over a pan of gently simmering water (ensuring the bowl doesn't touch the water underneath) and leave until just melted. Remove from the heat and set aside.

3. In a large bowl, beat the butter with an electric handheld mixer, then thoroughly mix in the icing sugar and cinnamon until creamy, about 3 minutes. Add the egg yolks, one yolk at a time, mixing well after each addition.

4. Add the melted chocolate when tepid, about 40°C/104°F, otherwise the egg yolks will cook. Stir to cool the melted chocolate and then add to the creamed mixture, stirring until just combined.

5. In a separate clean bowl, whisk the egg whites with clean beaters at medium speed until slightly thickened and foamy, about 2 minutes. Slowly add the granulated sugar and whisk until the egg whites hold soft peaks.

6. Using a rubber spatula, fold one-third of the whisked egg whites into the chocolate mixture, then gently fold in the rest until just incorporated. Fold in the cake flour, using a sieve to gradually and evenly distribute the flour over the top of the batter while you fold it in. Spread the batter evenly into the prepared cake tin and smooth the surface.

For the rum syrup
100g/3½oz/½ cup
   granulated sugar
120ml/4fl oz/½ cup water
2 tbsp rum (such as
   Austrian 60% Stroh
   Rum)

For the apricot filling
435g/15½oz/1½ cups
   smooth apricot jam (not
   jelly or preserves)

For the chocolate glaze
160g/5¾oz/scant 1 cup
   bittersweet or dark
   chocolate (75% cocoa
   solids), roughly chopped
110g/3¾oz/½ cup (1 stick)
   unsalted butter, diced

*For the 'schlag' (whipped
cream) for serving 12
portions*
950ml/scant 1¾ pints/
   4 cups double cream,
   well-chilled
2 tbsp icing sugar
1 tsp vanilla extract

7. Bake for 35–45 minutes or until a cocktail stick (toothpick) comes out clean when inserted into the centre of the cake or the internal temperature of the cake is 99°C/210°F. Remove from the oven and carefully flip the cake out of the tin onto the lined baking sheet. The perfectly flat bottom of the cake now effectively becomes the new even top of the Sachertorte. (If using, remove any baking paper from the tin that is attached to the cake.) Leave to cool for 20 minutes.

8. Meanwhile, make the rum syrup. In a small saucepan over a medium heat, stir the sugar into the water until it has dissolved. Stir in the rum, then remove from the heat and leave to cool.

9. Liberally brush the warm cake with the rum syrup, and reserve the remaining syrup for the next step. Once cool, cover the cake with clingfilm and refrigerate overnight.

10. The next day, carefully cut the cake in half horizontally using a long, serrated knife. Start by marking the cake all around and continue to slowly saw your way through the cake as horizontally as possible towards the centre from all sides. Brush the cake's cut sides generously with the reserved rum syrup.

11. Make the apricot filling. In a small saucepan, bring the apricot jam to the boil, stirring continuously, then immediately remove it from the heat. Leave it to cool until tepid, then spread one-third of the jam on top of the bottom layer of the cake. Place the other half of the cake on top and spread the remaining jam all over the top and sides of the cake. Refrigerate until set, about 2 hours.

12. Prepare the chocolate glaze. Gently melt the chocolate and butter together in a bain-marie (as before – see above). (To preserve the quality of the chocolate, it should only just melt, thus not exceed 50–55°C/122–131°F.) Remove from the heat when just melted and stir until smooth.

13. Place the cake on a wire rack set over a baking sheet. Stir the glaze while it cools to 32°C/90°F, then immediately pour the chocolate glaze over the centre of the cake. It should spread out evenly by itself, otherwise work quickly with a spatula to cover the cake completely. Refrigerate the cake until the glaze sets, about 5–10 minutes. Very carefully cut the bottom of the cake's glaze loose all around from the wire rack and transfer to a serving plate.

14. Make the 'schlag' (whipped cream). In a well-chilled bowl, whip the cream with an electric handheld mixer (or by hand using a balloon whisk), adding the icing sugar and vanilla. Whisk until the cream just thickens. (Take care not to over-whip the cream, which would render it grainy and buttery.)

15. To cut the cake for serving, dip a sharp knife into hot water between cutting each slice, wiping it dry with a piece of kitchen paper (paper towel). Serve each portion of the Sachertorte with a generous dollop of whipped cream and nothing else.

16. The cake can be stored in an airtight container in the fridge for up to 3 days.

Cook's Tip
• What to drink with the Sachertorte? Cognac, rum, and obviously coffee (especially a Kapuziner like Sigmund Freud liked) are traditional, but Sauterne and black tea are excellent, too.

Orly Ziv
Babka

This braided yeast cake with chocolate and halva is a favourite in the Jewish repertoire. I add crumbs of halva, a popular Middle Eastern sweet, to give the cake added texture and flavour.

Makes: 2 loaves/Serves 8 • **Prep time:** 30 minutes, plus rising/proving • **Cook time:** 25–30 minutes

For the dough

560g/1lb 4½oz/4¼ cups plain flour, plus extra for dusting

10g/¼oz/3½ tsp fast-action (easy-blend) dried yeast

100g/3½oz/½ cup caster or granulated sugar

100g/3½oz/scant ½ cup (7 tbsp) unsalted butter, softened

2 medium eggs

180ml/6¼fl oz/¾ cup whole milk

1 tsp salt

1 tsp vanilla extract

For the filling

about 400g/14oz chocolate spread (you can try Adeena Sussman's on page 110)

halva crumbs, for a generous sprinkling

1 medium egg, lightly beaten, to glaze

1. Line two 700g/1lb 9oz loaf tins with non-stick baking paper.

2. Put all the dough ingredients in a large mixing bowl and knead together by hand or in an electric stand mixer until a smooth and flexible dough is formed (see Tester's Tips). Cover loosely with a tea towel and leave to rise/prove until doubled in size. This will take a few hours, depending on how warm the room temperature is.

3. On a lightly floured surface, roll out the dough into a large rectangle about 0.5cm/¼in thick. Spread the chocolate spread for the filling over the dough, covering it completely, then sprinkle generously with halva crumbs. Roll the dough up lengthways into a tight log and press down slightly to seal. Cut the log in half, widthways.

4. Slice one of the log halves in half lengthways down the middle and then loosely twist the two halves together to form a plait (braid). Repeat with the second log of dough.

5. Transfer each plait to a lined loaf tin, shaping it to fit, then brush the top of each with beaten egg to glaze. Cover and set aside to rise/prove in a warm place for another 15 minutes.

6. Meanwhile, preheat the oven to 170°C/150°C fan/340°F/Gas Mark 3½.

7. Bake the babka for about 25–30 minutes, until golden. Remove from the oven and leave to cool in the tins for at least 20 minutes, then turn out onto a wire rack and leave to cool a little more before slicing. Serve warm or cold in slices.

8. Store the leftover babka (unsliced) in an airtight container at room temperature for a day or two.

Tester's Tips

• I also melted the butter and mixed the liquid ingredients together, the dry ingredients together, and then combined the two, which made it much easier to create a good, smooth dough. (DS)

• The dough initially needs to rise/prove for at least 3 hours. (DS)

Michael Solomonov
Chocolate-almond Situation

It's hard to believe this recipe is gluten-free! I especially love it as a great alternative to flourless chocolate cake. And it's very easy to make. Almond flour gives the cake fantastic structure while making sure it remains nice and moist – almost brownie-like in texture. The cake can be made ahead of time and cut into small cubes to serve with tea or coffee or cut into big wedges for dessert.

Serves: 8–12 (or more, if cut into small cubes) • **Prep time:** 25 minutes • **Cook time:** 30 minutes

vegetable oil, for greasing
315g/11oz/scant 2 cups
   dark chocolate (at least
   60% cocoa solids),
   roughly chopped
115g/4oz/½ cup (1 stick)
   unsalted butter, softened
200g/7oz/1 cup caster or
   granulated sugar
a big pinch of salt
4 large eggs, lightly beaten
55g/2oz/½ cup almond
   flour

1. Preheat the oven to 190°C/170°C fan/375°F/Gas Mark 5. Oil a 23cm/9in round or square cake tin, line the bottom with a piece of non-stick baking paper and oil the paper.

2. Melt the chocolate pieces in a heatproof bowl set over a pan of gently simmering water, ensuring the bottom of the bowl doesn't touch the water underneath. Remove from the heat and leave to cool slightly.

3. Combine the butter, sugar and salt in the bowl of an electric stand mixer fitted with the paddle attachment (or use an electric handheld mixer) and beat on medium-high speed until pale and fluffy, about 2 minutes.

4. Add the melted chocolate and mix just until combined. Scrape down the sides of the bowl with a spatula and mix for another few seconds. With the mixer on low speed, add the eggs, a little at a time, beating until each addition is incorporated before adding more.

5. Scrape down the sides of the bowl again, then add the almond flour and mix on low speed until just incorporated, about 10 seconds. Pour the batter into the prepared cake tin and smooth the top with a spatula (the batter will be very sticky).

6. Bake in the centre of the oven until a cocktail stick inserted in the centre of the cake comes out clean, about 25 minutes.

7. Remove from the oven and cool the cake in the tin for 10 minutes, then turn it out onto a wire rack and leave to cool completely. Serve in slices.

8. Store leftovers in an airtight container in a cool place for a couple or so days.

Tester's Tip
• You can dust the top with a little cocoa powder just before serving.

Savoury Dishes & Drinks

Denise Phillips
Sicilian Caponata

This is one of Sicily's popular dishes or side dishes, which is delicious served with fish or on top of bread like brochetta or bruschetta. Every home and restaurant has its own special twist and in Sicily, with nine provinces, there are nine regional variations. For example, Catania includes peppers, Palermo adds toasted pine nuts and Agrigento almonds, and Messina makes theirs Mexican-style with chocolate or cocoa powder! It is a vibrant mix of vegetables – and chocolate in this case!

The tradition is to make a big batch in advance and enjoy it cold – perfect for Yom Tov and Shabbat lunch.

Serves: 6 as a side dish • **Prep time:** 20 minutes, plus 1 hour to salt the aubergine • **Cook time:** 30 minutes

3 large aubergines (approx. 750g/1lb 10oz total weight)

salt, for sprinkling

vegetable oil, for frying

1 large onion, finely chopped

3 celery sticks, finely sliced

10 plum tomatoes, skinned and chopped

1 tsp light soft brown sugar

2 garlic cloves, finely chopped

3 tbsp stoned green olives, chopped

2 tbsp raisins

1 tbsp caper berries or capers in brine, rinsed

25g/1oz/⅙ cup dark chocolate (85% cocoa solids), roughly chopped

1 tbsp white wine vinegar

1 tsp salt

1 tbsp water

2 tbsp chopped fresh basil

To garnish

a few whole stoned green olives

a few basil leaves and extra chopped basil

freshly ground black pepper

1. Peel each aubergine in alternative strips lengthways (to get a stripy effect), then cut into 2.5cm/1in cubes. Place in a large colander, sprinkle with salt and set aside for 1 hour, then rinse and dry.

2. Add enough vegetable oil (about 2 tablespoons) to a large frying pan, then add some aubergine cubes (you'll need to do this in two or three batches) and fry over a medium heat until they are golden, turning regularly, about 5 minutes. Remove from the pan to a plate and set aside. Fry the remaining aubergine cubes in batches, adding extra oil for each batch, if needed.

3. In the same pan (in the residual oil left in the pan), sauté the onion and celery over a medium heat until just soft, about 4–5 minutes.

4. Stir in the tomatoes, sugar, garlic, olives, raisins, capers, chocolate, vinegar, measured salt and the fried aubergine cubes.

5. Add the water and simmer for 5–8 minutes to reduce the liquid and concentrate the flavours, stirring occasionally. Stir in the chopped basil.

6. Serve hot, warm or cold (personally, I like to serve it hot or warm).

7. To serve the stylish way, for each serving, place a small ring mould on a serving plate, spoon in some caponata to fill the mould, then lift up and remove the mould. Repeat for the remaining servings. Garnish each plate with olives, basil leaves, chopped basil and a dusting of black pepper. Alternatively, serve the caponata on one larger serving plate along with the garnishes.

8. The caponata will keep in an airtight container in the fridge for up to 3–4 days, then either serve it at room temperature or reheat it gently in a frying pan for about 5 minutes or until heated through, and stir in some extra chopped basil just before serving.

Ofer Vardi
Noodles with Cocoa

The Hungarian Dolce Vita: Hunyadi *Mátyás* was only 15 years old when he was crowned King of Hungary in 1458, and went on to be the greatest of Hungarian kings. He was a true renaissance man. He built castles and raised fortresses; he established libraries and published the first book of laws in the kingdom.

When he took Beatrix, daughter of the King of Naples, as his wife, the young princess brought a suitcase that, along with Versace dresses, was filled with onion and garlic, cheeses and, most importantly, pasta. All these ingredients caught on fast in Princess Beatrix's new homeland, especially the pasta – *tészta* or *metélt* in Hungarian.

Over the years, the number of new dishes made with prepared noodles increased. These were served as appetisers as well as main dishes and even dessert. Noodles with cabbage (*Káposztás Kocka*), noodles with cheese (*Túros Csusza*), and even noodles with nuts or with poppy seeds (*Mákos/Diós Metélt*). The *tészta* passed the test.

Grandma Nana made *Káposztás Tészta*, squares of soft pasta delightfully resting on a mound of hot cabbage that had caramelised slowly. Sometimes she served the noodles with nuts. And sometimes she scattered sweetened cocoa powder on top. *Mamma mia* – was it ever tasty! This is my version of noodles with cocoa, and it's also delicious!

Serves: 4 • **Prep time:** 10 minutes • **Cook time:** 10 minutes

4 litres/7 pints/17 cups water
1 tsp salt
400g/14oz/2 cups dried wide egg noodles
100g/3½oz/1 cup unsweetened cocoa powder
about 250g/9oz/1¾ cups icing sugar

1. Put the water and salt into a large saucepan and bring to the boil, then add the noodles and cook according to the packet instructions until tender.

2. Drain the noodles and transfer to a serving bowl.

3. Sift the cocoa powder and icing sugar together and mix. Add to the cooked noodles, toss together to mix well and serve.

Alan Rosenthal
Chocolate Chilli

I love making chilli con carne with whole pieces of chuck steak rather than minced (ground) beef; it makes it much more substantial and wholesome. Adding dark chocolate to the chilli also gives the dish a wonderful earthy richness that complements the mix of spices.

Serves: 6 • **Prep time:** 20 minutes • **Cook time:** 4 hours

3 tbsp olive oil
900g/2lb/4 cups beef
   chuck steak, cut into
   3–4cm/1¼–1½in pieces
2 onions, roughly chopped
3 garlic cloves, roughly
   chopped
1 cinnamon stick
½–1 tsp cayenne pepper
2 tsp dried oregano
2 tsp ground cumin
2 tsp ground allspice
4 dried (whole) chipotle
   chillies
1 x 400g/14oz tin chopped
   tomatoes
60g/2¼oz/4 tbsp tomato
   purée
2 tbsp maple syrup or
   runny honey
1 red pepper, deseeded
   and roughly chopped
1 green pepper, deseeded
   and roughly chopped
500ml/18fl oz/generous
   2 cups water
1 x 400g/14oz tin red kidney
   beans, drained and rinsed
20g/¾oz dark chocolate
   (at least 70% cocoa
   solids), chopped
salt and freshly ground
   black pepper
fresh lime juice
fresh coriander
hot cooked rice

1. Preheat the oven to 160°C/140°C fan/325°F/Gas Mark 3.

2. Heat the olive oil in a heavy-based, flameproof casserole dish that has a lid over a medium-high heat, and brown the pieces of beef for 3–4 minutes in batches. Once well browned, transfer to a bowl.

3. Add the onions to the casserole and cook over a medium heat until soft and translucent, about 10 minutes. Stir in the garlic, cinnamon stick, cayenne pepper, oregano, cumin, allspice and chipotle chillies and cook for a couple of minutes, adding a little more oil if it feels too dry.

4. Next, add the tomatoes, tomato purée, maple syrup or honey, red and green peppers and water. Mix everything well and season liberally with salt and pepper. Stir in the browned meat, together with any juices that have collected, and bring to a simmer. Pop the lid on, transfer the casserole to the oven and cook for 3 hours, stirring once halfway through.

5. After the long wait, stir in the kidney beans, then return the casserole to the oven for about 30 minutes with the lid off. Once the chilli has thickened, stir in the chocolate until melted, then taste and adjust the seasoning.

6. Serve with a squeeze of fresh lime, a little chopped coriander scattered over and some fluffy cooked rice alongside.

Cook's Tips
• If you can't find chipotle chillies, don't worry, simply replace them with a teaspoon of smoked paprika.
• This chilli will keep well in an airtight container in the fridge for up to 3 days – simply transfer the hot chilli to a suitable container and cool it quickly, then cover and refrigerate. To serve, reheat gently in a saucepan on the hob until piping hot throughout. It also freezes well for up to 6 months (defrost in the fridge overnight before reheating as above).

Curaçao Hot Chocolate

It's hard to beat a mugful of this warming and delicious hot chocolate. It's like a hug in a mug! Together with the Panlevi, this is a must at every *Brit Milah* (circumcision ceremony).

Serves: 4 • **Prep time:** 10 minutes • **Cook time:** 5–10 minutes

1 x 410g/14½oz tin
  evaporated milk
3½ tbsp unsweetened
  cocoa powder, plus extra
  (optional) to serve
4 tbsp granulated sugar (or
  to taste)
a pinch of salt
1 tsp vanilla extract
1 medium egg

1. Place all the ingredients, except the egg, in a saucepan. Fill the empty evaporated milk can with water and add this to the pan. Mix well and bring gently to the boil, stirring constantly.

2. Remove from the heat and cool to drinking temperature.

3. Beat the egg well, then add to the cocoa mixture, stirring to combine.

4. Pour into serving mugs/cups and serve immediately with an extra sprinkle of cocoa powder on top, if you like.

Panlevi

This is one of the most ancient, but also one of the most popular, recipes of the Curaçao Sephardim. Traditionally baked for all holidays and other festive occasions, these crisp sponge cookies are often sent to relatives and the sick, and they are essential served with the Curaçao Hot Chocolate.

Makes: 4 • **Prep time:** 25 minutes • **Cook time:** 20 minutes

vegetable oil, for greasing
3 medium eggs, beaten
100g/3½oz/½ cup
  granulated sugar
a pinch of salt
¼ tsp ground cinnamon
½ tsp vanilla extract
100g/3½oz/¾ cup plain
  flour, plus extra for
  dusting
½ tsp baking powder

1. Preheat the oven to 180°C/160°C fan/350°F/Gas Mark 4. Grease and lightly flour two large baking sheets.

2. Put the eggs, sugar, salt and cinnamon into a mixing bowl and beat together well, either by hand or using an electric handheld mixer, then stir in the vanilla. Fold in the flour and baking powder by hand to make a smooth batter.

3. Drop tablespoonfuls of the cookie batter onto the prepared baking sheets, spacing them about 5cm/2in apart.

4. Bake for 10 minutes, then reduce the oven temperature to 140°C/120°C fan/275°F/Gas Mark 1 and bake for another 5 minutes or until the cookies are lightly browned.

5. Remove from the oven and loosen the cookies from the baking sheets using a palette knife. Turn the oven off, then return the cookies to the oven to crisp up. Once crisp, transfer to a wire rack and leave to cool. Serve with Curaçao Hot Chocolate (see above).

6. Store the panlevi in an airtight container at room temperature – they should keep for a few days.

Cook's Tip
• For a stronger flavour, double the amount of ground cinnamon and vanilla extract in the recipe. (DP)

Claudia Roden
Thick Hot Chocolate Drink – *Chocolate a la Taza*

Thick, creamy, rich hot chocolate served with *churros* (long, ribbed, crisp dough fritters) is a popular breakfast in Spain. *Chocolaterías* specialise in the drink, which is made with dark bitter chocolate and a little cornflour to thicken the milk. The amount of sugar needed depends on the sweetness of the chocolate.

Serves: 2 • **Prep time:** 5 minutes • **Cook time:** 10 minutes

2 tsp cornflour
500ml/18fl oz/generous
   2 cups whole milk
115g/4oz/1¼ cups grated
   good-quality bittersweet
   or dark chocolate
2–3 tsp granulated sugar,
   or to taste

1. In a small bowl, dissolve the cornflour in 2 tablespoons of the cold milk.

2. Bring the rest of the milk to the boil in a saucepan, then pour in the cornflour mixture, stirring with a wooden spoon.

3. Cook over a low heat for 2–3 minutes, stirring until the milk thickens slightly and becomes creamy.

4. Remove from the heat, add the grated chocolate and keep stirring until it has melted entirely, then stir in the sugar to taste. Pour into mugs or cups to serve.

Tester's Tips
- Be patient! It might take the milk more than 3 minutes to thicken.
- Gentle heat works best here: make sure the milk isn't boiling when you add the chocolate and add the chocolate gradually. (RD)

Claudia Prieto Piastro
Mexican *Chocolate al Agua*

Chocolate al agua is the most popular breakfast drink in Oaxaca. You can find *molinos* (grinders) all over Oaxaca city and the markets are full of stalls offering this drink. Preparing hot chocolate by grinding it in a *metate* and dissolving it in water is a pre-Hispanic tradition, the addition of sugar came later on with the Europeans. Although originally it was a ritual drink, during the colonial period it became popular, especially among Spanish women.

Serves: 16 • **Prep time:** 25 minutes, plus 1 hour soaking and chilling • **Cook time:** 10–15 minutes

125g/4½oz/1 cup raw cacao nibs
8g/¼oz cinnamon sticks
3g/⅛oz dried allspice berries
250g/9oz/1¼ cups granulated sugar
1 litre/1¾ pints/1 quart boiling water, to serve

1. Put the cacao nibs in a bowl and cover with cold water. Leave them to soak for at least 1 hour (I don't leave for longer than 2 hours). Drain the nibs.

2. Heat a dry cast-iron or heavy-based pan over a medium heat. Arrange the cacao nibs in the pan in a single layer. Toast them for around 10 minutes or until you can smell the chocolate. You might need to do this in batches. Once toasted, tip out onto a plate and leave to cool completely, then remove any shells (if they had any).

3. Meanwhile, in the same pan, toast the cinnamon sticks and allspice berries until they release their aroma, about 1–1½ minutes. Remove from the heat.

4. Grind the cinnamon, allspice and cacao nibs together until they become a paste. Traditionally, this is done in a *metate* (horizontal mortar made with volcanic rocks), but you can do this in a grinder, a powerful food processor or by hand in any mortar. If you do this by hand, be aware that it will take around 30 minutes at least, and start with the spices followed by the cacao nibs.

5. Mix the cacao paste with the sugar and knead together for a few minutes.

6. Press the paste together into compact balls or use silicone moulds to make small chocolate bars. Transfer to a plate (if making balls) and allow them to chill in the fridge for about 3 hours. The balls/bars will keep in an airtight container in the fridge for up to 2 months.

7. To make Mexican hot chocolate (to serve four people), dissolve 90g/3¼oz of the paste in the boiling water. Mix constantly with a Mexican *molinillo* or a hand whisk until the paste is completely dissolved and the hot chocolate is frothy. Serve hot with brioche or challah.

Cook's Tip
• In markets in Oaxaca, this *chocolate al agua* is served for breakfast with a bread roll known as *pan de yema* (egg yolk bread) that is similar in texture to challah. If you want to get closer to this bread, add fennel or anise seeds to your bread dough.

Hot & Cold Desserts

Claire Berson
Chocolate Soup

For all those chocoholics out there, indulge yourself with this ultimate chocolate dessert. This soup will wow your dinner party guests and will satisfy your chocolate cravings. This recipe is not exactly low in calories, but a small serving of dark (preferably organic) chocolate is actually good for you. It is full of antioxidants, which can help protect the body from aging, high blood pressure, high cholesterol and heart disease. Have I convinced you yet?

Serves: 6 • **Prep time:** 10 minutes • **Cook time:** 10–15 minutes

250ml/9fl oz/generous 1 cup water
100ml/3½fl oz/generous ⅓ cup whipping cream
1 tbsp icing sugar
2 tbsp organic unsweetened cocoa powder, sifted
100g/3½oz/scant ⅔ cup organic dark chocolate (60–70% cocoa solids), broken into pieces

To decorate
roasted flaked almonds
a few fresh red berries, such as blueberries, raspberries or strawberries (use 3 strawberries, hulled)
1 tsp Crème de Cassis (optional)
icing sugar, for dusting

1. This soup will be ready to serve within 10 minutes and has to be served immediately. Therefore, start with roasting the flaked almonds for the decoration, or you can use pre-toasted flaked almonds, if you prefer. Prepare the fruit for the decoration – rinse the fruit and pat dry, then slice the strawberries (if using).

2. To make sure the chocolate doesn't burn, make this soup in a bain-marie. Place a heatproof bowl over a pan of gently simmering water – the bottom of the bowl should sit above the water without touching it.

3. Add the water, whipping cream, sugar and cocoa powder to the heatproof bowl. Whisk it together for 3–5 minutes.

4. Add the chocolate pieces to the mixture. Keep stirring and allow the chocolate to melt so that the mixture becomes smooth and shiny – it should be a little bit thicker than hot chocolate.

5. Stir in the Crème de Cassis (if using), then pour the lukewarm soup into small coffee/espresso cups to serve.

6. Decorate each cupful with the prepared red berries of your choice and the roasted flaked almonds. Sprinkle a little icing sugar on top and serve immediately.

Cook's Tip
• To toast the almonds, preheat the oven to 180°C/160°C fan/350°F/Gas Mark 4. Spread the almonds out in a single layer on a baking sheet. Roast for 3–4 minutes, then shake the baking sheet to stir the almonds. Return to the oven (if needed) for a further few minutes, checking every minute, until they're golden brown. Remove from the oven, immediately tip onto a plate and leave to cool.

Liz Alpern and Jeffrey Yoskowitz
Dark Chocolate and Roasted Beet Ice Cream

Something about the sweetness of beets and their deep crimson colour feels so in line with the Ashkenazi dessert tradition, although I doubt that Jews from Dubienka were experimenting with vegetable-flavoured ice creams. This recipe, originally published in *The Gefilte Manifesto: New Recipes for Old World Jewish Foods*, can also be made without the mint if that's not your thing.

Makes: about 600ml/20fl oz/2½ cups ice cream
Prep time: 25 minutes, plus chilling, churning and freezing ● **Cook time:** 1 hour 5 minutes – 1 hour 25 minutes

250g/9oz whole raw beetroots/beets (about 3 medium), scrubbed
120ml/4fl oz/½ cup, plus 2 tbsp whole milk
120ml/4fl oz/½ cup double cream
4–5 fresh mint sprigs, leaves picked (optional)
2 large egg yolks
50g/1¾oz/¼ cup caster or granulated sugar
55g/2oz/⅓ cup dark chocolate, broken into pieces

To decorate
dark chocolate shavings
small fresh mint sprigs

1. Preheat the oven to 200°C/180°C fan/400°F/Gas Mark 6. Wrap the beetroots individually in foil and place them on a baking sheet. Roast for 40–60 minutes or until they are fork-tender.

2. Remove from the oven and set aside to cool. When cool enough to handle, peel the beetroots (the skin should peel off easily under cold running water). Quarter them, then place in a blender with 2 tablespoons of milk and blend until smooth. To remove any remaining solids, pass the mixture through a fine-mesh sieve lined with four layers of wet muslin (cheesecloth). Set aside.

3. In a small saucepan, combine the remaining milk, the cream and mint (if using) and heat over a low heat. Using the bottom of a clean jar or glass, muddle the mint into the milk-cream mixture to release its flavours. Cook over a low heat, stirring occasionally, for about 15 minutes.

4. Meanwhile, in a small, heatproof bowl, whisk together the egg yolks and sugar until light in colour and just combined, then set aside. If using mint, remove the leaves from the milk-cream mixture with a slotted spoon.

5. Slowly pour a couple of tablespoons of the hot milk-cream mixture into the sugar-egg mixture, whisking continuously, then pour the sugar-egg mixture back into the pan of hot milk-cream mixture to make a custard. Increase the heat to medium-low and stir continuously until it thickens and turns a pale yellow, about 10 minutes. Do not let the custard boil. The custard is ready when it coats the back of a spoon. Remove from the heat, pour into a medium, heatproof bowl and leave it to cool slightly.

6. Meanwhile, melt the chocolate in a separate heatproof bowl set over a pan of gently simmering water, ensuring the bottom of the bowl doesn't touch the water underneath. Remove from the heat and stir the melted chocolate into the custard, then stir in the beetroot liquid.

7. Place the chocolate-beetroot ice cream base into an airtight container or your ice-cream maker's canister, cover with a lid or clingfilm and refrigerate until chilled, at least a couple of hours or up to overnight.

8. Once chilled, churn the ice cream base in your ice-cream maker according to the manufacturer's instructions. Store the finished ice cream in the freezer (it's best eaten within a month of freezing); transfer it to the fridge 15–20 minutes before serving to soften it a bit.

Cook's Tips

• If you don't have an ice-cream maker, you can use the 'freeze and stir' method. Pour the chilled ice cream base into a shallow bowl, dish or container, cover and place it in the freezer. Every 30–45 minutes, remove the container from the freezer and stir vigorously for a minute or two, then re-cover and place back in the freezer. Repeat this process over a 4-hour period. Serve the ice cream right away or cover and store in the freezer until you're ready to enjoy it.

• This ice cream is delicious and perfect served on its own, but it is also good served in a waffle cone, to add a little salty crunch at the end.

Leticia Moreinos Schwartz
Molten Brigadeiro Cakes (*Bolinho Quente de Brigadeiro*)

Brigadeiro is the national candy of Brazil. With the size of a truffle and the taste of fudge, Brazilians are wild about them. One bite may be all it takes for you to quickly count them among your favourite indulgences as well.

To make these molten cakes, I took the brigadeiro in its fudge state and developed the recipe to become an irresistible flow of melted fudge, since so many Brazilians (including me) can't even wait until their brigadeiro is cool before indulging. My experimentation turned into a great recipe!

A word of advice about these molten cakes: butter and flour the foil containers or ramekins really well. It's so frustrating when a cake doesn't come out of the container properly and part of it is left behind. So don't rely on a thin coating of grease spray; use soft butter – not melted – and shake off the excess flour.

Serves: 6 • **Prep time:** 25 minutes • **Cook time:** 20 minutes

For the brigadeiro

1 x 400g/14oz tin sweetened condensed milk

1 tsp unsweetened cocoa powder

60g/2¼oz/⅓ cup dark chocolate (70% cocoa solids), roughly chopped

For the cake

115g/4oz/½ cup (1 stick) unsalted butter, plus extra for greasing

2 large whole eggs, plus 2 large egg yolks

⅛ tsp salt

1 tbsp caster or granulated sugar

1 tsp vanilla extract

40g/1½oz/generous ¼ cup plain flour, plus extra for dusting

ice cream (pistachio, ginger, coconut or vanilla are all flavours that work well with this dessert), to serve

1. Preheat the oven to 180°C/160°C fan/350°F/Gas Mark 4. Butter and flour six individual 175g/6oz/¾ cup foil cups/containers or ramekins (see intro).

2. Make the brigadeiro. Place the condensed milk, cocoa powder and chocolate in a heavy-based saucepan and bring to the boil over a medium heat, whisking constantly. When the mixture begins to bubble and the chocolate melts, reduce the heat to low and continue whisking for another 3–5 minutes, until the mixture has thickened like fudge and is bubbling like lava. You should be able to tilt the pan and the whole fudgy batter will slide, leaving a sticky residue on the bottom of the pan. Slide the fudgy batter into a large, heatproof bowl without scraping the pan. You don't want to incorporate any of the thick residue on the bottom of the pan (just discard this). Set aside.

3. Prepare the cake mixture. Melt the butter in a separate small saucepan over a low heat. Pour into the brigadeiro and whisk vigorously until smooth. At first the mixture will totally curdle and break. You will think this recipe cannot possibly work, but keep whisking constantly until the mixture comes together again and is emulsified.

4. In a separate bowl, beat together the eggs, egg yolks, salt, sugar and vanilla. Add this into the brigadeiro mixture and whisk until combined. Sift in the flour and mix in with a spatula, just until blended.

5. Pour the cake mixture into the prepared foil cups/containers, filling them almost to the top (leave about 5mm/¼in space at the top). You can prepare the recipe up to this point and refrigerate for up to 5 days.

6. Place the foil cups/containers on a baking sheet. Bake for 7–9 minutes or until the edges are firm but the centre is still soft. Remove from the oven, then invert each cake onto a dessert plate, carefully releasing it from the foil cup/container. Serve with ice cream.

Cook's Tips

- If you are making these in advance, either cover each filled foil cup/container with clingfilm or place the filled foil cups/containers inside a large airtight container and close the lid, then refrigerate.
- They can then be cooked from chilled, but you will need to add an extra 1–2 minutes to the total cooking time given above (or, bring them to room temperature before baking as above).
- I like to serve these with ice cream, but fresh fruit and whipped cream are also good accompaniments.

Amir Batito
Cream Cheese and Nutella Blintzes

These blintzes are the perfect comfort food! Easy to make and easy to eat! In these crazy times, we all need some sweet treats for the soul. Batter, cream cheese and chocolate (Nutella) will definitely do the trick.

Makes: 8 blintzes • **Prep time:** 25 minutes • **Cook time:** 15–20 minutes

For the blintzes
2 medium eggs
35g/1¼oz/¼ cup plain
   flour
3 tbsp whole milk
1 tbsp melted unsalted
   butter
1 tbsp caster or granulated
   sugar
sunflower oil, for frying

For the stuffing
250g/9oz/generous 1 cup
   cream cheese
4 tbsp caster or granulated
   sugar
1 tsp vanilla extract
8 tsp Nutella

1 tbsp unsalted butter, to
   serve

Tester's Tip
• Double-up the blintzes mixture, if you prefer, to make slightly thicker pancakes, otherwise you need to make the crêpes extremely thin! This makes a perfect Shavuot treat, when it is traditional to have dairy foods. (ML and NM)

1. To make the blintzes, place all the ingredients, except the sunflower oil, in a bowl and whisk together until smooth and combined.

2. Heat a little sunflower oil in a large frying pan (skillet) over a medium heat and once it's very hot, pour an eighth of the batter into the hot pan, so that a thin layer covers the entire surface of the pan. After about a minute, when the mixture dries and a thin crêpe is formed, use a spatula to turn it over, then brown it on the other side for another 30 seconds or so. Transfer the cooked blintz to a plate and repeat the process with the rest of the mixture, to make a total of eight blintzes.

3. For the stuffing, place the cream cheese, sugar and vanilla in a bowl and mix together well. Using a spoon, add a little of the cream cheese mixture to the centre of each blintz, and then, next to the mixture, add a teaspoonful of Nutella. Fold both sides of each blintz over the stuffing, then carefully roll up from one open/unfolded side to the other to enclose the filling and make a rolled-up parcel.

4. Melt the butter (to serve) in a clean frying pan over a medium heat, then add the blintzes (you may need to do this in a couple of batches, depending on the size of your pan) and sear for about 1 minute on each side, until golden. Serve hot.

Michael Daniel
Chocolate Fondant with Prunes in Armagnac

This is one of those dishes in which several flavours that are wonderful in their own right blend together to produce something remarkable. Digging your spoon into this pud reveals a mass of gooey chocolate that is as alluring as it is tasty. You can make one big pudding instead of the small ones, but it will take longer to cook – about 15 minutes. Don't serve more than a fifth of this pud to anyone or use the mix to make less than five small puddings, as it is so rich and dense they won't be able to finish it!

Serves: 5–6 • **Prep time:** 25 minutes, plus overnight soaking • **Cook time:** 17 minutes

about 8 good-quality, stoned (pitted) dried prunes, roughly chopped

50ml/2fl oz/scant ¼ cup Armagnac

350g/12oz/2½ cups good-quality dark chocolate (minimum 70% cocoa solids), finely chopped

100g/3½oz/scant ½ cup (7 tbsp) unsalted butter, at room temperature, diced

150g/5½oz/¾ cup caster or granulated sugar

4 medium eggs

55g/2oz/scant ½ cup plain flour

a pinch of salt

1. Well ahead, ideally the night before, soak the prunes in the Armagnac.

2. Preheat the oven to 230°C/210°C fan/450°F/Gas Mark 8. Line five or six small (individual) ovenproof pudding bowls or large ramekins with foil.

3. Melt the chocolate in a large, heatproof bowl set over a pan of gently simmering water (ensuring the bottom of the bowl doesn't touch the water underneath). Remove from the heat.

4. In another large bowl, beat the butter and sugar together until the colour of the mixture goes pale. Beat in the eggs, one at a time, making sure that each one is well amalgamated before adding the next. Finally, sift in the flour with the salt and mix in well.

5. Mix one-third of the butter, sugar and flour mixture into the melted chocolate until combined. Add this back to the bowl of remaining butter/sugar/flour mixture and fold in lightly with a metal spoon until uniform in colour. Stir in the prunes and any remaining unabsorbed liquid.

6. Spoon the mixture into the prepared bowls or ramekins, dividing it evenly – they shouldn't be much more than half full. Bake for about 12 minutes, until the top of each looks baked and is cracking in several places. Don't cook for any longer, otherwise the filling will not be nice and gooey.

7. Remove from the oven and cool for 1 minute or so before serving. To serve, gently loosen and ease each dessert out of its foil-lined dish and invert onto a serving plate.

Tester's Tip
• The prunes are very boozy! If I made this again, I might cut the booze with some other non-alcoholic liquid to dial down the shock of the alcohol! You could try replacing some of the Armagnac with a quick, simple sugar syrup (1:1) infused with some cinnamon and other warm spices, or just use plain water, or perhaps some unsweetened orange juice. (NG)

Bonbons, Bites & After-Dinner Delights

Anya von Bremzen
Chocolate-covered Cheese Confections

These rich, chocolate-covered cheese confections, sold in the dairy department in Soviet grocery shops, used to be a favourite childhood treat. It took a little trial and error to come up with a homemade version, but it was worth it just to get the happy smile of recognition from my Russian friends and compliments from my American guests.

Makes: about 25 balls • **Prep time:** 25 minutes, plus chilling/freezing and setting • **Cook time:** 5 minutes

350g/12oz/1½ cups curd cheese or small-curd cottage cheese (farmer's cheese)

115g/4oz/½ cup cream cheese

90g/3¼oz/scant ½ cup (7 tbsp) granulated sugar

2 large egg yolks, lightly beaten

grated zest of 2 lemons

1½ tsp lemon extract

1 tbsp fresh lemon juice

240g/8¾oz/scant 1½ cups bittersweet or dark chocolate (at least 60% cocoa solids), broken into pieces

3 tbsp solid (white) vegetable shortening, diced

1. In a food processor, combine the cheeses, sugar and egg yolks and process until completely smooth. Transfer to a bowl and stir in the lemon zest, lemon extract and lemon juice.

2. Tip the mixture into a double thickness of damp muslin (cheesecloth), wrapping it around the mixture, then place in a colander set over a bowl to allow the liquid to drain away. Fold the ends of the muslin over the top. Place a small plate on top of the muslin and put a 900g/2lb weight, such as a large (filled) food tin, on the plate. Refrigerate overnight.

3. The next day, discard the liquid in the bowl. Unwrap the cheese mixture, then divide and form it into 4cm/1½in balls with your hands. Place the balls on a plate and freeze to firm up, about 30 minutes.

4. Meanwhile, place the chocolate and shortening in a heavy-based saucepan and melt over a low heat, stirring constantly. Remove from the heat and allow the chocolate to cool to lukewarm.

5. Line a large plate with non-stick baking paper. Remove the cheese balls from the freezer. Insert a cocktail stick into the centre of one ball and dip it into the chocolate, coating it completely and allowing the excess to drip back into the pan. Place on the lined plate and remove the cocktail stick, then dab a small amount of chocolate over the little hole left behind. Repeat with the rest of the cheese balls. Refrigerate until the chocolate has set.

6. Store these confections in an airtight container in the fridge for up to 2 days.

Cook's Tip
• Decorate the chocolates with melted white chocolate instead for extra effect – simply replace the dark chocolate with good-quality white chocolate and melt as above, then cool and coat the cheese balls.

Linda Dangoor
'No Bake' Chocolate, Tahina and Nut Truffles

These truffles are very easy and fun to make. I find that Lindt baking chocolate (51% cocoa solids) has a good balance of sweet and bitter flavours (aim for at least 50% cocoa solids baking chocolate). The tahina (tahini) gives a creamy smoothness to them and the scant pinch of paprika leaves a warm spicy feeling in the mouth right at the end.

Makes: about 40 small balls • **Prep time:** 25 minutes, plus chilling and setting • **Cook time:** 5 minutes

100g/3½oz/scant ⅔ cup
  Lindt baking chocolate
  (51% cocoa solids),
  broken into pieces
3 tbsp Menier (100%)
  unsweetened cocoa
  powder, plus extra for
  dusting
60g/2¼oz/½ cup walnuts,
  finely ground
60g/2¼oz/½ cup whole
  almonds, finely ground
40g/1½oz/⅓ cup cashew
  nuts, finely ground
3 tbsp tahina (tahini)
⅛ tsp paprika
sesame seeds, for coating

1. Place the chocolate pieces in a heatproof bowl set over a pan of gently simmering water, ensuring the bottom of the bowl doesn't touch the water underneath, and heat until melted.

2. Remove the bowl from the heat. Add the cocoa powder, all the ground nuts, the tahina and paprika to the melted chocolate and mix to make a smooth dough. Cover and leave to rest in the fridge for an hour or so, to stiffen up a little. After resting, if the dough is too wet, mix in an extra ½ tablespoon (or a little more) cocoa powder.

3. Take little pieces of the dough and shape into small balls (you will make about 40 in total). Roll them first in the sesame seeds (for more texture), then in some extra cocoa powder, covering them completely. Arrange the truffles in a single layer on a flat serving dish. Leave them for a few hours to firm up at room temperature or place them in the fridge before serving.

Cook's Tips
• These truffles will taste better the following day. They also keep well in an airtight container, either at room temperature or in the fridge, for at least a month (if they last that long!).
• The recipe can easily be halved, if you prefer.

Linda Dangoor
Chocolate and Date Nuggets

To make these delicious nuggets, I found that different brands of cocoa powder gave different results, as did different varieties of dates.

The first time, I used Green & Black's unsweetened cocoa powder and an Iranian soft date variety. The result was mediocre. I found the flavour quite bitter notwithstanding the sweetness of the dates. My guinea-pig friends and my husband, however, loved them. The next time I made them, I changed the proportion of chocolate to dates and nuts. The flavour improved, but was still not spot-on for my palate.

For my third try, I changed to Medjool dates because of their current availability in most supermarkets. I also changed the brand of cocoa powder to a French brand called Menier (also available in many supermarkets). Surprisingly, it made all the difference. The nuggets were delicious with the right amount of bitterness and sweetness.

Undoubtedly, the variety of the chocolate beans and the way they are roasted contributes to their flavour. So, in conclusion, although both powders are 100% cocoa, the Menier brand is not as bitter and is my favourite for making these dessert nuggets.

Makes: about 30 balls • **Prep time:** 25 minutes, plus chilling • **Cook time:** 12 minutes

2 Medjool dates, about 40g/1½oz, stoned (pitted)

40g/1½oz/⅓ cup whole almonds

40g/1½oz/⅓ cup walnuts

30g/1oz/2 tbsp dark soft brown sugar

1 large egg white or 2 medium egg whites, lightly whisked with a fork until bubbles form

2 tbsp Menier (100%) unsweetened cocoa powder, plus extra for dusting

¼ tsp ground cardamom (optional)

rose water or cold water (for wetting fingers for shaping dough)

1. Pulse the dates in a food processor, then add the almonds, walnuts and sugar and pulse until finely chopped and well combined. Tip into a bowl. Alternatively, finely chop the dates and walnuts and roughly chop the almonds using a sharp knife, then mix with the sugar in a bowl.

2. Add the lightly whisked egg whites, cocoa powder and ground cardamom (if using). Mix together well with a spoon and then with your fingers. The dough should have body. If it's too wet, add an extra ½ teaspoon of cocoa powder. Cover and leave to rest in the fridge for a few hours or overnight.

3. Preheat the oven to 180°C/160°C fan/350°F/Gas Mark 4. Line a baking sheet with non-stick baking paper.

4. Have a bowl with a little rose water (or cold water) in for wetting your fingers. Wet your fingers very lightly, take little portions of the dough, each a little smaller than the size of a walnut, and shape into rough balls. Arrange them on the lined baking sheet. Space the balls out as they might expand when baked.

5. Bake for about 12 minutes or so, until a golden brown tinge appears. Remove from the oven and leave to cool a little. If some of them are out of shape, adjust them while they are still warm and roll them in extra cocoa powder to coat. Place them on a serving dish and wait for the balls to cool completely before serving.

Linda Dangoor
Chocolate and Coconut Bonbons

I have put my twist on this traditional Indian recipe, which uses condensed milk instead of eggs. I have added pure cocoa powder to the milk, turning the bonbons into milk chocolate treats with a dusting of cardamom and bitter cocoa powder on top to give them an edge. The cardamom is optional.

Makes: about 35–40 bonbons • **Prep time:** 25 minutes • **Cook time:** 15 minutes

1 x 297g/10½oz tin sweetened condensed milk

2 tbsp Menier (100%) unsweetened cocoa powder (or of your choice), plus extra for dusting

200g/7oz/2 cups desiccated (dried unsweetened shredded) coconut, plus 1 tbsp extra for dusting

1 tsp ground cardamom, for dusting (optional)

1. Pour the condensed milk into a heavy-based pan and place it over a medium-low heat. Mix in the cocoa powder, smoothing out any lumps, and stir continuously. When the mixture heats up and starts to gently bubble, add the coconut and mix vigorously. Continue mixing and folding for about 10 minutes until you get a more solid consistency that you will be able to roll. Be careful not to burn the mixture.

2. When you are satisfied with the consistency, remove from the heat and tip it into a heatproof bowl, then wait for the dough to cool down a little.

3. Spread some extra coconut over your work surface. Take about a teaspoonful of the dough and roll it into a ball with your palms, then into the coconut to coat. Depending on the size of your bonbons, you should make about 35–40.

4. Sprinkle each bonbon with a little cardamom (if using) and a little of the extra cocoa powder, then transfer to a serving plate and place in the fridge to firm up slightly. Serve at room temperature.

Cook's Tip
• These bonbons will keep in an airtight container in the fridge for a month or so (if they haven't been devoured beforehand!).

Rachel Davies
Tahini Chocolate Bark

Tahini is such a versatile ingredient. Traditionally, it's used to make tahini sauce and hummus, but it can be used in sweet and savoury dishes and is irresistible in desserts, especially with chocolate!

In developing this recipe, I was inspired by The Good Egg, an Israeli-style restaurant in London that serves a divine chocolate bark for dessert. They top theirs with rose petals or sour cranberries and halva and also with candied orange, sesame seeds and pine nuts.

Making chocolate bark is a lovely way of putting your own stamp on something very simple – some dried fruit or nuts, definitely some sea salt, and you can get creative with the rest. A little piece with a hot drink after dinner is a lovely way to finish a meal.

Serves: about 12–16 • **Prep time:** 25 minutes, plus chilling/setting • **Cook time:** 10 minutes

200g/7oz/1½ cups good-quality dark chocolate (at least 70% cocoa solids), finely chopped
135g/4¾oz/1 cup white chocolate, finely chopped (I just use Milky Bar buttons!)
90g/3¼oz/scant ½ cup tahini
1 tsp vanilla extract
½ tsp sea salt flakes
120g/4¼oz/½ cup double cream

Toppings of your choice, such as:
dried sour cherries, cranberries, freeze-dried raspberries, edible dried rose petals
pistachio nibs, chopped toasted pecans, salted almonds
broken-up pieces of halva
black or white sesame seeds, puffed rice, dried coconut flakes
sea salt flakes

1. Line a medium-sized cake tin with non-stick baking paper, cutting enough paper to go just up the sides of the tin as well – I use a brownie tin for this, which is about 25 x 17cm/10 x 6½in.

2. Melt the dark chocolate in a heatproof bowl set over a pan of barely simmering water (a bain-marie), ensuring the bottom of the bowl doesn't touch the water underneath. Stir until smooth, then remove the bowl from the pan (being careful as it will be hot) and set aside.

3. Place the chopped white chocolate in a separate heatproof mixing bowl with the tahini, vanilla and salt flakes. Set aside.

4. Gently heat the cream in a small saucepan until it is just boiling. Turn off the heat and wait a minute or a little longer if the cream is really hot, before pouring the cream onto the white chocolate. Wait another minute and then stir until you have a smooth and creamy ganache. If the chocolate is lumpy, you can hold the bowl over the bain-marie briefly and stir again. White chocolate will split if exposed to a high heat so be cautious!

5. Pour the tahini ganache into the lined tin, spreading it evenly over the base. Spread melted dark chocolate over the top and swirl together with a knife.

6. Sprinkle over the toppings of your choice, and leave to set for at least 2 hours in the fridge. Break into pieces to serve.

7. If not enjoying immediately, transfer to an airtight container and store in the fridge for up to 1 week or in the freezer for up to 3 months. Eat from chilled or frozen.

Clarissa Hyman
Delicias aka Almond and Chocolate 'Delights'

Delicias: Almond and chocolate 'delights'. An understatement. This recipe comes from Valencia, the great orange garden of Spain. In April and May, the trees are as pretty as spring brides, and the intense perfume of the blossom intoxicating. Later in the year, the groves between the mountains and the sea are ablaze with luminous fruit and shiny leaves of baize-green. These petit fours always remind me of the best fruit of all – the one you eat straight from the tree.

Makes: 24 'delights' • **Prep time:** 30 minutes, plus 1 hour chilling • **Cook time:** 5 minutes

100g/3½oz/scant ⅔ cup dark chocolate (around 70% cocoa solids), broken into pieces
30g/1oz/2 tbsp (¼ stick) unsalted butter, diced
1 tbsp single cream or creamy whole milk
125g/4½oz/generous ¾ cup icing sugar
4 tbsp fresh orange juice
190g/6½oz/scant 2 cups ground almonds

1. Line a baking sheet with non-stick baking paper or greaseproof paper.

2. Melt the chocolate pieces, butter and cream or milk together in a bain-marie (a heatproof bowl set over a pan of gently simmering water, ensuring the bottom of the bowl doesn't touch the water underneath), stirring occasionally until the mixture forms a thick coating sauce. Remove from the heat and set aside.

3. In a separate mixing bowl, stir together the icing sugar and orange juice until smooth, then add the ground almonds. Mix until the paste feels slightly sticky and starts to hold together in clumps. Add a little more orange juice, if necessary.

4. Pinch off small pieces of the almond mixture and use your hands to shape, squeeze and roll each piece into a small, smooth ball. Dip each one in the chocolate sauce until well coated (hands are also best for this, aided perhaps by a spoon, so expect sticky fingers) and place on the prepared baking sheet, leaving a little space between each one. Once they are all dipped, chill in the fridge for at least an hour until the coating is firm.

5. Place each one in a ruffled paper case before serving. Store in an airtight container at room temperature for a day or two (if the weather is very hot or you need to keep them a little longer, store them in the fridge, but whenever I make them, they don't last that long!).

Aviva Elias
Chocolate Cardamom Truffles

Chocolate truffles are an ultimate indulgence. I adapted a recipe with flavours that I enjoy, so I hope you enjoy it, too.

Makes: around 18–20 truffles • **Prep time:** 20 minutes, plus chilling • **Cook time:** 5–10 minutes

150ml/5fl oz/⅔ cup double cream
30g/1oz/2 tbsp unsalted butter
375g/13oz/scant 2¼ cups dark chocolate (60% cocoa solids), chopped
1 tsp vanilla extract
2 tbsp light soft brown sugar
¼ tsp ground cardamom
2 pinches of Himalayan Pink salt (or other sea salt)
3 tbsp unsweetened cocoa powder

1. Heat the cream and butter together in a saucepan over a low heat until the butter has melted. Add the chocolate pieces and stir gently until melted and combined.

2. Add the vanilla, sugar, cardamom and salt and stir well over the heat, just until the sugar dissolves and combines, then remove from the heat.

3. Pour the mixture into a heatproof bowl and leave to cool, then cover and refrigerate for at least 2 hours or overnight until firm.

4. Put the cocoa powder into a small bowl. Gently divide and roll the chilled chocolate mixture into walnut-sized balls, then drop each one into the cocoa powder and roll to coat. Transfer to a plate and serve, or pack in a small presentation box. Serve at room temperature.

5. These truffles should be stored in an airtight container in a cool place but not in the fridge as this will dampen the cocoa coating. They will keep for up to 7–10 days (if they last that long).

Cook's Tip
• Cardamom can be substituted with ground ginger or cinnamon or chilli powder, if you like. Or better still, make a batch of each!

Tester's Tips
• The truffle mix is a delightful basis for experimenting with different flavours. You can add in the cardamom right at that last moment on the heat (or instead you can use ground ginger, chilli powder, extra salt, rose extract or other things from a Sephardi palate, or perhaps try lemon, lime, mint or mango extract for a western taste).
• Or you can add flavour to the cocoa powder – I have a delicious spicy Mexican cocoa powder that I used on some of the chocolate cardamom truffles to excellent effect. (DF)

Adeena Sussman
Olive Oil Chocolate Spread

Israel's own *Hashachar Ha'Oleh* ('Rising Dawn'), a cheap sugar rush of spreadable chocolate originally created as a way to get calories into young Israelis for breakfast or after school, used to give Nutella a run for its money. But its base of cheap chocolate and vegetable oil has caused it to suffer a bit of bad PR in recent years. For a kid, the parent-endorsed idea of being able to spread chocolate on any sort of supporting vehicle (my favourite: matzah) holds massive appeal – and it still does for adults (well, at least this adult). This is my version, made with good-quality chocolate, olive oil, cocoa powder and a healthy amount of salt. You can use any kind of chocolate you like, from milk to dark, and you need to refrigerate it after cooking for an initial firming up.

Serves: 8 • **Prep time:** 15 minutes, plus chilling • **Cook time:** 5 minutes

80ml/2¾fl oz/⅓ cup water
130g/4¾oz/⅔ cup
  granulated sugar
2 tbsp unsweetened cocoa
  powder
½ tsp kosher salt
175g/6oz/1 cup
  bittersweet, semi-sweet
  or dark chocolate,
  roughly chopped
60ml/4 tbsp/¼ cup extra
  virgin olive oil
1 tsp vanilla extract
matzah, to serve
flaky sea salt, such as
  Maldon, for sprinkling

1. In a small saucepan, bring the water, sugar, cocoa powder and kosher salt to the boil over a medium heat.

2. Reduce the heat to medium-low and cook, whisking until the sugar has dissolved and the mixture thickens, about 2–3 minutes.

3. Remove the pan from the heat and whisk in the chocolate, olive oil and vanilla until the chocolate is melted and smooth.

4. Transfer to a heatproof bowl, press a piece of clingfilm onto the surface of the chocolate mixture, cool slightly, then refrigerate until thick but spreadable, about 2 hours.

5. Remove from the fridge to soften for 30 minutes, or microwave on medium for about 10 seconds, then stir before serving. Spread on matzah and sprinkle with flaky sea salt, then serve.

6. Store the chocolate spread in an airtight container in the fridge for up to 2 months.

Gabrielle Rossmer Gropman and Sonya Gropman
Spiced Chocolate Hazelnut Cookies (*Krokerle*)

These are chocolate-spiced cookies with yummy roasted hazelnuts, iced with a sweet-tart lemon glaze. The recipe, from Herta and Marion Bloch, is traditionally baked by their family as a Hanukkah treat. The Christmas cookie tradition in Germany is widespread and includes many varieties. It is so pervasive, as both a seasonal and a cultural tradition, that it was naturally adopted by Jews. There are innumerable varieties of spice cookies (with the most famous being *Lebkuchen*), and *Krokerle* fall into this category.

Makes: approximately 45–65 cookies • **Prep time:** 35 minutes • **Cook time:** 20–25 minutes

sunflower oil, for greasing (optional)

For the cookies
225g/8oz/1¾ cups whole hazelnuts (with skin on)
4 large eggs
300g/10½oz/1½ cups granulated sugar
360g/12½oz/2¾ cups plain flour
1½ tsp baking powder
1 tsp ground cloves, cinnamon, nutmeg or mixed spice
25g/1oz/¼ cup unsweetened cocoa powder
50ml/2fl oz/scant ¼ cup brandy or whisky

For the lemon glaze
210g/7½oz/1½ cups icing sugar, sifted
1½ tbsp fresh lemon juice

1. Preheat the oven to 180°C/160°C fan/350°F/Gas Mark 4. Line three baking sheets with non-stick baking paper or grease with sunflower oil.

2. For the cookies, spread the hazelnuts out on one of the lined baking sheets and toast in the oven for about 10 minutes or until you start to smell them. Be careful not to let them burn. Immediately remove them from the oven and spread out on a clean tea towel. Leave the oven on and set the lined baking sheet to one side – for baking the cookies. Wrap the four corners of the tea towel over the top of the nuts and leave them to sit for a few minutes. The steam will help to loosen the nut skins. Roll the nuts around in the tea towel – most will become skinless. Coarsely chop and set aside.

3. Whisk together the eggs and sugar in a bowl until light and foamy.

4. In a separate bowl, sift together the flour, baking powder, spice and cocoa powder. Stir the dry ingredients into the egg and sugar mixture. Add the brandy or whisky and the chopped hazelnuts and stir to combine.

5. Drop teaspoonfuls of the mixture onto the prepared baking sheets, spacing them about 5cm/2in apart. Bake in the oven for 10–15 minutes or until lightly browned. Remove from the oven, then transfer to a wire rack to cool.

6. For the lemon glaze, combine the icing sugar and lemon juice in a bowl and stir until smooth. Add a few drops of water if the glaze is too thick.

7. While the cookies are still warm, drizzle each one with a spoonful of the glaze. Leave to cool completely. Store in an airtight container.

Tester's Tips
• For a richer, deeper flavour use muscovado or dark brown sugar instead of granulated, and add 1 tsp each of cinnamon and ginger, ½ tsp mixed spice or allspice and a generous pinch of sea salt to the flour mixture. (JR)
• If you like lemon glaze, make double the amount so you have enough to drizzle over all the cookies. (NW)

Adam Kendler
Milk Chocolate Fudge

This melt-in-the-mouth fudge recipe only takes 45–50 minutes to make and then it's just a matter of patience waiting for it to set, but trust me, it's well worth the wait! The fudge will keep for up to a month in an airtight container in the fridge... but I'd be surprised if it lasts that long!

Makes: about 1kg/2lb 4oz fudge (which cuts into 50–55 x 2.5cm/1in cubes)
Prep time: 25 minutes, plus setting and chilling • **Cook time:** 25 minutes

vegetable oil, for greasing
225g/8oz/1 cup (2 sticks) unsalted butter
180g/6¼oz evaporated milk
500g/1lb 2oz/2½ cups caster or granulated sugar
a dash of vanilla extract
180g/6¼oz/1 cup milk cooking chocolate, broken into pieces

1. Grease a 20cm/8in square baking tin that is at least 4cm/1½in deep, with vegetable oil and line with non-stick baking paper.

2. Put the butter, evaporated milk and sugar in a heavy-based saucepan and cook over a medium heat, stirring occasionally so the butter doesn't separate, until melted and the sugar has dissolved.

3. Stir in the vanilla, then bring to the boil over a high heat – but do not stir with a wooden spoon, just leave the fudge alone! Use a sugar thermometer to periodically measure the temperature, but do not touch the base of the pan with the thermometer.

4. Once the mixture has reached 116°C/241°F, remove from the heat and carefully pour into a heatproof bowl (preferably metal, or a heavy-duty plastic one) of an electric stand mixer. Add the chocolate, then let it just sit for 30 seconds to melt.

5. Now mix on a constant low speed for 8–12 minutes, using a spatula to scrape around the sides of the bowl occasionally. When the fudge is ready, the mixture should form solid ripples around the mixer beaters and the spatula should come out clean when touching the fudge. You can do this by hand using a wooden spoon if you don't have a stand mixer, but it will take a lot longer (15–20 minutes) and requires lots of elbow grease!

6. Once the fudge mixture is firm enough, pour it into the lined baking tin. Allow the fudge to cool at room temperature for 3–5 hours, then cover and refrigerate for at least another 2 hours.

7. Using a pizza cutter, cut around the sides of the tin, invert the tin and turn the fudge out onto a chopping board. Cut into 2.5cm/1in cubes and serve.

Marlena Spieler
Chocolate Matzos

I set about concocting this treat in an effort to gather the flavours of both East and West in one little Passover goody: thin, crisp, caramelised toasted matzos (ancient Jewish traditional flatbreads), with a thick layer of dark chocolate, a hit of sea salt and the Asian flavour of crystallised ginger. Fresh rosemary boosts the ginger, but it is not necessary. If you keep kosher, you'll notice it's pareve, that is, it may be eaten with either a dairy or meat meal. Use the best chocolate you can find, of course.

    This recipe is inspired by and loosely based on the caramel and chocolate-covered matzos that make the rounds each Pesach. Adding the aromatic extras, and freezing it into a crisp, cold treat, is pretty wonderful and adds to their charm.

Serves: 12 • **Prep time:** 15 minutes, plus freezing • **Cook time:** 8 minutes

3 tbsp extra virgin olive oil (plus a little extra, if needed)

4–6 matzos (in the UK, sold as flame-baked crackers/flatbread)

about 110g/3¾oz/ generous ½ cup light soft brown sugar

several pinches of sea salt flakes

250g/9oz/1¾ cups bittersweet or dark chocolate (60–70% cocoa solids), finely chopped

55–85g/2–3oz crystallised ginger, coarsely chopped (or to taste)

1 tbsp finely chopped fresh rosemary (optional)

1. Preheat the oven to 200°C/180°C fan/400°F/Gas Mark 6.

2. Drizzle a tiny amount of the olive oil over a baking sheet, preferably a non-stick one. Break up the matzo squares and place on the baking sheet in a single layer. Drizzle with the remaining olive oil, then sprinkle evenly with the brown sugar and rub the sugar into the matzo pieces.

3. Bake for about 8 minutes – if your oven runs hot, check after 6 minutes; if it runs low, go the whole 8 minutes or longer if needed. You can also grill the matzos under a high or medium-high heat – watch them like a hawk – but the bottom won't get toasty the way it does with baking. After baking, the matzos should look (unevenly) golden and toasted and the olive oil/sugar should be caramelised.

4. Remove from the oven and as soon as it comes out of the oven, sprinkle with the sea salt, then the chocolate. Spread if the chocolate melts readily; if it doesn't, place back in the oven for about 30 seconds or long enough for the chocolate to become soft and spreadable.

5. Sprinkle the ginger and rosemary (if using) over the top, then set aside until cool to the touch. Freeze the matzos on the baking sheet for at least 3 hours to harden the chocolate. Once frozen, transfer them to an airtight container or tightly wrap them in foil and return to the freezer. Serve from frozen.

6. These will keep in the freezer for several weeks.

Cook's Tip
• Use 4 matzos if using the larger ones from the US, Israel and other countries; use 5–6 matzos if using UK ones (which are smaller).

Leah Koenig
Chocolate-dipped Figs

Lots of fruits get dipped in chocolate – strawberries, cherries, apricots – but none of them compete with a chocolate-dipped fig. There is just something magical that happens when you combine the dried fruit's jammy sweetness and light crunch of seeds with a layer of bittersweet or dark chocolate. They are also ridiculously simple to make, while making a big impact – as in, bring them to a party and you will immediately become the life of it.

Serves: 4 • **Prep time:** 15 minutes, plus 15 minutes chilling • **Cook time:** 5 minutes

55g/2oz/⅓ cup bittersweet or dark chocolate, roughly chopped
12 dried Calimyrna figs
flaky sea salt, for sprinkling

1. Line a large baking sheet with non-stick baking paper.

2. Melt the chocolate in a heatproof bowl set over a pan of gently simmering water, ensuring the bottom of the bowl doesn't touch the water underneath. Or melt it in the microwave in a microwave-safe bowl on medium for 30-second bursts, stirring after each burst, until fully melted.

3. Use your fingers to reshape any figs that have got flattened in their package.

4. Dip the rounded bottom half of each fig in the melted chocolate and then lay them on their sides on the prepared baking sheet. Sprinkle each chocolate-coated fig bottom with a little sea salt.

5. Refrigerate the figs until the chocolate sets, about 15 minutes. Serve chilled or at room temperature. Store in an airtight container in the fridge.

Cook's Tips
- The sprinkle of sea salt brings everything together, so don't skip it!
- Dried Calimyrna figs are caramel-coloured and have a deep, sweet flavour. If you cannot find them, substitute Turkish Smyrna figs or smaller, darker dried Black Mission figs, or your favourite variety.

Victoria Prever
Chocolate Peppermint Macaroon Kisses

My son adores mint choc chip ice cream, as do I. So, when inventing a new Pesach recipe, I decided those flavours may just work to pep up the (let's face it) slightly dull, annual macaroon. The result was chewy, crunchy and different. If you don't like mint, replace it with orange zest or just stick with dark chocolate.

Makes: 16 macaroon kisses • **Prep time:** 35 minutes, plus setting • **Cook time:** 20 minutes

2 large egg whites
200g/7oz/1 cup caster or granulated sugar
45g/1¾oz/½ cup unsweetened cocoa powder, sifted
a few drops of peppermint extract
225g/8oz/2¼ cups ground almonds
85g/3oz/½ cup dark chocolate, broken into pieces
½ tsp flavourless oil (such as sunflower oil)

1. Preheat the oven to 180°C/160°C fan/350°F/Gas Mark 4. Line two baking sheets with non-stick baking paper. Have a bowl of cold water ready to dampen your hands.

2. Whisk the egg whites in a clean mixing bowl until stiff. Gradually add the sugar and whisk for 2–3 minutes until very thick.

3. Whisk in the sifted cocoa powder and peppermint extract until combined. Carefully fold in the ground almonds and mix until completely combined. The batter will be thick and sticky.

4. With damp hands, shape 1 heaped teaspoonful of the almond mixture into a 2cm/¾in ball, then pinch to form it into a teardrop shape. Place on one of the lined baking sheets.

5. Leaving about 4cm/1½in between each almond teardrop, continue to shape the teardrops until all the mixture is used up (you will make 32 teardrop shapes). Dipping the teaspoon into water before scooping will help to ease the mixture off the spoon. Wipe excess water off the spoon after dipping, or things get messy!

6. Bake until slightly cracked, about 12–15 minutes. Remove from the oven and leave to cool on the baking sheets for a couple of minutes before transferring them to a wire rack. They will be soft but will firm up as they cool. If you cook them too much they will be too hard when they cool.

7. For the coating, melt the chocolate with the oil in a bain-marie. Alternatively, melt the chocolate and oil together in a microwave-safe bowl on medium in 30-second bursts, stirring after each burst.

8. Spoon a little of the melted chocolate onto the flat side of one macaroon cookie and then place another cookie, flat-side down, on top. Press them together and leave on the wire rack to let the chocolate harden. Repeat with the remaining cookies. Once the chocolate sets, they are ready to serve.

Cook's Tip
• You can dust the kisses with a little icing sugar, just before serving, if you like.

Judi Rose
Jewelled Chocolate and Pomegranate Discs

These indulgent, easy-to-make chocolate discs, with their irresistible mix of smooth dark chocolate, crunchy nuts and tangy fresh pomegranate seeds, are a rather beautiful after-dinner treat and healthy alternative to a box of chocolates.

Dark chocolate contains polyphenols that can help to prevent heart disease, cancer and Alzheimer's disease. Pomegranate seeds are rich in antioxidants and help control blood pressure, while nuts are a good source of protein, healthy fats and vitamins B and E.

Mixing melted and unmelted chocolate together – a process known as tempering – changes the structure of the chocolate, giving the finished discs a lovely glossy finish. Feel free to add other toppings like goji berries, sultanas, rose petals, and flaked sea salt. To make chocolate *gelt*, gild the finished discs with edible gold spray or lustre dust.

Makes: 12–14 discs • **Prep time:** 15 minutes, plus setting • **Cook time:** 5 minutes

100g/3½oz/scant ⅔ cup good-quality dark (70%+ cocoa solids) chocolate chips or finely chopped bars

50g/1 ½ oz/scant ½ cup shelled pistachios and chopped pecans

1. Line a baking sheet with non-stick baking paper.

2. Set a heatproof bowl over a pan of barely simmering water, making sure the bottom of the bowl doesn't touch the water. Add two-thirds of the chocolate and stir until almost melted.

3. Add the remaining third of unmelted chocolate to the bowl, remove from the heat and stir vigorously for a minute or two until smooth. If it's still lumpy, reheat over the hot water or microwave on full power in 10-second bursts.

4. Working quickly before the chocolate starts to set, drop teaspoonfuls of the melted chocolate onto the baking paper, spreading each into a 5cm/2in circle with the back of your spoon. Stud each disc with the nuts and pomegranate seeds (or other toppings of your choice). Leave to set, but don't refrigerate or the chocolate will lose its gleam.

Cook's Tips
• Because of the fresh pomegranate, the discs are best eaten the same day. If you want to keep them longer or give them as an edible gift, use dried fruit instead of the pomegranate seeds and they'll keep up for up to 1 week in an airtight container. To make chocolate bark instead of discs, spread the melted chocolate in a 1cm /½in thick layer then add the toppings as before.
• As a shortcut, use a 100g/3½oz packet of giant dark chocolate buttons instead of a chocolate bar. Soften them slightly in the microwave, then arrange them on a lined baking sheet and add the toppings as before. The chocolate won't stay glossy but will taste fine.

Fabienne Viner-Luzzato
Homemade After-Dinner Mints

These homemade after-eights are so moreish! They are very easy to make, they'll help you to digest and will also impress your guests!

Makes: 25 pieces (depending on size) • **Prep time:** 20 minutes, plus chilling • **Cook time:** 5 minutes

250g/9oz/1½ cups dark chocolate (at least 65% cocoa solids), broken into pieces

210g/7½oz/1½ cups icing sugar, plus a little extra if needed

2 tbsp water

2–3 tsp peppermint extract (or to taste)

1. Line a 23cm/9in baking tray (with shallow lipped edges) with non-stick baking paper or use a disposable foil tray of the same size.

2. In a microwave-safe bowl, heat the chocolate pieces on medium in 30-second bursts, until fully melted, stirring after each burst. Alternatively, melt the chocolate in a heatproof bowl set over a pan of gently simmering water (ensuring the bottom of the bowl doesn't touch the water underneath).

3. Pour half of the melted chocolate into the prepared baking tray and spread into a thin, even layer. Leave to cool and set in the fridge until firm. Set the remaining melted chocolate aside at room temperature.

4. In a mixing bowl, mix the icing sugar, water and peppermint extract together until it forms a thick, smooth paste. If the mixture is too thick, add a bit more water; if it is too thin, add a bit more icing sugar.

5. Spread the peppermint mixture evenly over the top of the cooled chocolate. Refrigerate for about 15 minutes or until firm.

6. Pour the remaining melted chocolate over the peppermint mixture and spread into a thin, even layer. If the chocolate has begun to set, just re-melt it briefly as before.

7. Refrigerate until fully set, about 1 hour, or if you are in a hurry, put it in the freezer. Once fully set, break into pieces and serve.

8. Store the pieces in an airtight container in the fridge – they will keep for up to 3 days (but they won't last that long, they are too good!).

Silvia Nacamulli
Chocolate Salami

This is the first dessert I ever made as a young child and it is still one of my all-time favourites. I used to make it together with my older brother and sister on Sunday mornings while my parents were still asleep. Being the youngest, I was not allowed to do that much, so I ended up cleaning all the bowls, which I didn't mind as that was the tastiest bit (and still is!).

The original recipe for the dessert comes from a classic children's recipe book called *Il Manuale di Nonna Papera* (*The Manual of Grandma Duck*). This recipe is very similar to the original version, with a little less biscuit and no alcohol. You can add a sweet liqueur to give it a kick and make it richer in flavour, or you can add mixed dried fruit (such as chopped dates or apricots), or nuts to the biscuits.

It is great sliced and served chilled. Do not leave at room temperature for more than 15–20 minutes. Children will love both making and eating it… and adults, too! Please note this recipe contains raw eggs.

Serves: 6–8 for dessert/Makes about 25–30 slices (depending on thickness)
Prep time: 20 minutes, plus freezing

150g/5½oz/⅔ cup (1¼ sticks) unsalted butter
2 large egg yolks
2 tbsp caster or granulated sugar
2 tbsp unsweetened cocoa powder
a pinch of salt
200g/7oz dry tea biscuits, such as Rich Tea

1. Melt the butter in a small pan over a low heat, or in a microwave-safe bowl in the microwave on medium in short bursts.

2. Meanwhile, put the egg yolks and sugar into a mixing bowl and beat together by hand, or using an electric handheld mixer, until you have a smooth and creamy consistency. Once the butter has melted, add it to the egg and sugar mixture, stir well, then add the cocoa powder and salt and mix.

3. Break the biscuits into small pieces and then add to the chocolate mixture. Work the mixture with your hands and mould/roll it to create a salami shape roughly 30cm/12in long. Wrap it in greaseproof paper, then wrap again in foil and place it in the freezer for at least 2 hours.

4. Take the chocolate salami out of the freezer 10 minutes before serving and remove the foil and greaseproof paper, then slice it fairly thinly.

5. This chocolate salami will keep (wrapped) in the freezer for several weeks so you can just cut yourself a slice whenever you feel like a sweet treat...

Tester's Tips
• I added a dash of amaretto to the chocolate salami mixture too!
• You can cover/sprinkle the top of the frozen roll with sifted icing sugar to make it look even more like salami. (NH)

Cook's Tips
• If you are using salted butter there is no need to add the pinch of salt.
• A good way to break the biscuits is to wrap them in a tea towel and bash it a few times, or to put them in a freezer bag and bash it with a rolling pin. Alternatively, cut them a few at a time with a sharp knife into about 0.5cm/½ in pieces.
• Make sure you wrap the salami shape in greaseproof paper and foil, as clingfilm may split when frozen.

Sevim Zakuto
Gatosalam

This is a Turkish Sepheradic recipe, which my grandmother and my mother used to make, and I learnt to make it at the age of 12. It's a simple and very comforting dessert; my mother made it at events, while I made it at pyjama parties with my friends. It can also be served as a sweet snack between meals and is great with tea or coffee.

Makes: 18–20 slices • **Prep time:** 20 minutes, plus freezing • **Cook time:** 5–10 minutes

100g/3½oz/scant ⅔ cup
   dark chocolate
   (preferably 60–70%
   cocoa solids), broken
   into pieces
125g/4½oz/generous
   ½ cup (1⅛ sticks)
   unsalted butter or pareve
   margarine, diced
2½ tbsp unsweetened
   cocoa powder
2 tbsp caster or granulated
   sugar
250g/9oz plain butter
   biscuits, such as petit
   beurre
60g/2¼oz/½ cup mixed
   roasted nuts and raisins
1 medium egg, beaten
2 tbsp desiccated (dried
   unsweetened shredded)
   coconut, to decorate

1. Place the chocolate, butter or margarine, cocoa powder and sugar in a heatproof bowl set over a pan of gently simmering water (ensuring the bowl doesn't touch the water underneath) and leave until melted and combined, stirring occasionally. Remove from the heat, then leave to cool to room temperature.

2. Break the biscuits into 1cm/½in chunks (not crumbs) and mix with the roasted nuts and raisins in a separate bowl.

3. Mix the beaten egg into the cooled melted-chocolate mixture until incorporated. Finally, fold in the biscuit mixture until combined, making a fairly firm dough that can be shaped, then tip the dough onto a sheet of non-stick baking paper. Wrap the baking paper around the dough to enclose it, rolling it into a salami shape, about 5–7cm/2–2¾in width/thickness.

4. Once shaped, wrap the paper-wrapped roll in clingfilm or foil and freeze for a minimum of 6 hours, until firm. Remove from the freezer at least 1 hour before serving, then roll the 'salami' in the desiccated coconut to lightly coat. Cut into slices, each about 2.5cm/1in thick, and serve.

5. Once sliced, keep in an airtight container in the fridge for up to 3 days, or keep the undecorated 'salami' roll in the freezer for up to 2 months.

Cook's Tips
• I also make this recipe using dark orange chocolate (70% cocoa solids) and it's excellent, too!
• If you cannot find petit beurre biscuits, try using other crisp, buttery biscuits instead.
• Instead of using desiccated coconut to decorate, try using crushed or finely chopped nuts (almonds, hazelnuts, pistachios), and add a little finely grated orange zest to the nuts to add extra flavour, if you like.

Judi Rose and Evelyn Rose
Hamantaschen with Chocolate and Poppy Seeds

Purim (the Feast of Lots) commemorates the downfall of Haman, the evil vizier of King Ahasuerus of Persia who planned to massacre the local Jewish community. According to the story, Haman drew lots to decide which day to carry out his plan. However, he ended up on the gallows he had prepared for his enemies, and his notoriety is perpetuated in a variety of three-cornered cookies – some say they are like the shape of his vizier's hat, others his purse which he planned to fill with Jewish gold, represented by poppy or sesame seeds.

Our recipe features a meltingly tender pastry which is especially easy to handle – it's the one Sephardi cooks use to make their wonderful melt-in-the-mouth moulded filled cookies like *ma'amouls*. When filled with an Ashkenazi poppy seed filling, and enriched with dark chocolate, a bite of these hamantaschen is truly a *mechia* (a special treat).

Makes: about 20 hamantaschen • **Prep time:** 25 minutes, plus cooling and chilling • **Cook time:** 30 minutes

For the filling
125g/4½oz/1 cup poppy seeds
125ml/4fl oz/½ cup whole milk or water
30g/1oz/2 tbsp (¼ stick) unsalted butter, cut into small cubes
50g/1¾oz/¼ cup soft brown sugar
1 tbsp maple syrup or runny honey
2 tbsp sultanas or raisins
30g/1oz good-quality dark chocolate, finely chopped, or dark chocolate chips
50g/1¾oz/½ cup ground almonds
1 tsp vanilla extract
a pinch of fine sea salt

For the pastry
225g/8oz/1¾ cups plain flour, plus extra for dusting
a pinch of fine sea salt

1. First, make filling. Grind the poppy seeds in a nut- or coffee-grinder, then place in a saucepan with all the other filling ingredients and heat gently, stirring constantly, until a very thick paste is formed that leaves the bottom of the pan clean when stirred, about 5 minutes. Remove from the heat, transfer to a bowl and leave to cool.

2. Meanwhile, make the pastry. Put the flour and salt into the bowl of a food processor with the well-chilled butter. Pour the cold water and orange blossom water or lemon juice/water mixture into the bowl, pulsing until the mixture looks like a moist crumble, then tip it into a bowl and gather it together to form a dough. Press the dough into a slightly flattened disc, then wrap it in clingfilm and chill in the fridge until the filling is cold and you're ready to make the hamantaschen.

3. Preheat the oven to 190°C/170°C fan/375°F/Gas Mark 5. Line two baking sheets with non-stick baking paper.

4. Unwrap the chilled dough and roll it out on a lightly floured work surface to a thickness of 3mm/⅛in. Cut the pastry into about 20 circles, each about 7.5cm/3in in diameter (an empty, well-washed tuna can makes an ideal cutter, or just use a round biscuit cutter).

5. Put a heaped teaspoonful of the cooled filling in the centre of each pastry circle, then bring the edges of each up and over the filling to form a triangle, pinching them together with your fingers to ensure a tight seal but leaving a gap in the centre of each to allow steam to escape. Place on the prepared baking sheets, leaving a space between each one.

150g/5½oz/⅔ cup (1¼
   sticks) unsalted cold
   butter, cut into small
   cubes

2 tbsp cold water

1 tbsp orange blossom
   water, or 2 tsp lemon
   juice and 2 tsp extra cold
   water

1–2 tbsp icing sugar, for
   dusting

6. Bake for 25 minutes or until firm when gently touched, but uncoloured. Remove from the oven, transfer to a wire rack and leave to cool for 10 minutes, then lightly dust with icing sugar. When quite cold, lightly dust them again, then serve.

7. Store any leftovers in an airtight container at room temperature for up to a week, or freeze for up to 3 months (defrost before serving).

Cook's Tips
- To make the pastry without a food processor, simply sift the flour and salt into a bowl, then lightly rub in the cubes of butter until the mixture resembles breadcrumbs. Add the cold water and orange blossom water or lemon juice/water mixture and mix to a dough, then shape, wrap and chill as above.

Glossary of UK–US Terms

Aubergine	Eggplant
Baking sheet	Unrimmed cookie sheet
Baking tin	Sheet pan or jelly roll pan
Bicarbonate of soda	Baking soda
Biscuits	Cookies
Bramley apples	Use a mix of Braeburn, Granny Smith, Northern Spy or Winesap
Bread flour	All-purpose flour
Cake tin	Cake pan
Caster sugar	Regular white sugar
Clingfilm	Plastic wrap
Cocktail stick	Toothpick
Coriander (fresh)	Cilantro
Cornflour	Cornstarch
Dark chocolate	Plain chocolate
Double cream	Heavy cream
Enamelled casserole	Dutch oven
Extra-strong bread flour	Bread flour
Foil	Aluminum foil
Icing sugar	Confectioners' or powdered sugar
Plain flour	All-purpose flour
Purée	Paste
Rapeseed oil	Canola oil
Skimmed milk	1% milk
Self-raising flour	Self-rising flour
Sieve	Strainer
Single cream	Light cream
Sultanas	Golden raisins
Tin	Can

A Note on Measurements

Both UK metric/imperial and imperial US cup measurements are included in these recipes for your convenience. Conversions are approximate and may have been rounded up or down. It is important to follow one set of measurements only and not alternate between them within a recipe, as they are not interchangeable.
All spoon measurements are level. 1 teaspoon is 5ml; 1 tablespoon is 15ml.

Egg sizes given in recipes are medium (UK) = large (US), or large (UK) = extra-large (US).

Ovens should be preheated to the specified temperature (check with an oven thermometer). Electric conventional (non-fan) and fan oven temperatures are included, but do check with your manufacturer's instructions when using a fan oven.
The total prep times and cook times given in the recipes are just a guide.

Contributors

Kenden Alfond

Kenden Alfond is a psychotherapist who started Jewish Food Hero as a community service project. When she was 12 years old, she chose to become a vegetarian (and is now 99% vegan). In 2005, she went to India as an American Jewish World Service (AJWS) volunteer and went on to live and work in Afghanistan, Democratic Republic of Congo, Switzerland and Cambodia, working on various projects for the United Nations and NGOs.

In 2013, Kenden obtained a certificate in plant-based nutrition from Cornell University, US. She started Jewish Food Hero to get healthier food onto Jewish tables around the world. Check out her plant-based and vegan cookbooks: *The Jewish Food Hero Cookbook: 50 Simple Plant-based Recipes*; *Feeding Women in the Bible, Feeding Ourselves* and *Beyond Chopped Liver: 59 Jewish Recipes Get a Vegan Health Makeover*. You can follow Kenden on Instagram and Twitter at @jewishfoodhero or visit www.jewishfoodhero.com

Liz Alpern and Jeffrey Yoskowitz

Liz Alpern and Jeffrey Yoskowitz are co-founders of The Gefilteria, a new kind of food venture launched in 2012 with a manifesto and a mission to reimagine eastern European Jewish cuisine. Together, they authored a narrative cookbook, *The Gefilte Manifesto: New Recipes for Old World Jewish Foods*. In addition to producing a celebrated artisanal gefilte fish, Alpern and Yoskowitz travel the world (and the virtual world) empowering communities through food. You can follow them on social media @gefilteria

Amir Batito

Born and raised in Israel, Amir has been fascinated by cooking ever since he was a little boy. He still cannot say who was a better cook – his mum or his grandma – but they both taught him a lot. After travelling the world, Amir returned to Israel and studied pastry in Israel's largest culinary school.

Though he started out as a pastry chef, Amir was soon drawn to the other side of the kitchen. After working with the Machneyuda group, followed by launching one of Israel's finest boutique hotels, Amir settled in the UK and has worked with renowned companies such as Jamie Oliver and Tony Page.

After a while, Amir opened his own catering company called Maghreb, which provides a wonderful way to connect to people, exploring and discovering new flavours. You can follow Amir on Instagram at @maghrebldn or go to www.maghreblondon.co.uk

Amy Kritzer Becker

Amy Kritzer Becker is the founder of the modern Jewish cooking blog What Jew Wanna Eat and author of the 2016 cookbook *Sweet Noshings*. She is also the owner of the cool Jewish gifts website ModernTribe (https://moderntribe.com).

After a stint in New York City as a conference producer, Amy moved to Austin, Texas, to escape the cold weather. Soon after, Amy left the business world to attend culinary school to work on her true passion. As she worked as a personal chef and did live cooking demos and classes at a supermarket, her blog grew and gained recognition.

Amy has had the opportunity to develop recipes, such as Avocado Latkes, Breakfast Tacos and Pumpkin Fig Rugelach for numerous publications, and she has spoken on the topics of culture, entrepreneurship and food at events around the world, like SXSW and Nosh Berlin. Amy and her recipes have been featured in *The New York Times*, *The Wall Street Journal*, *NPR*, *The Today Show* (NBC), *Food & Wine* and more. In autumn 2017, she appeared on an episode of *Guy's Grocery Games* on The Food Network.

Amy lives in Puerto Rico with her husband. You can follow her on Instagram and Twitter at @whatjewwannaeat or visit whatjewwannaeat.com

Claire Berson

Claire Berson is a UK-based food writer who has loved eating soups for as long as she can remember. Claire shares her passion for soup and recipes on her website www.ilovesoup.net

Anya von Bremzen

Moscow-born food writer, Anya von Bremzen, is the winner of three James Beard Awards for her books and journalism. She is the author of six acclaimed cookbooks including *Paladares*, her latest book about Cuba, as well as a memoir, *Mastering the Art of Soviet Cooking*, which has been translated into eighteen languages.

Anya has written for *Food & Wine*, *Travel + Leisure*, *Saveur*, *The New Yorker*, and *Foreign Policy* magazines among other publications. A contributing writer to *AFAR* magazine, she divides her time between Queens, New York, and Istanbul. You can follow her on Instagram and Twitter at @vonbremzen

Martyne Burman

Despite Martyne's family being a mix of Ashkenazi and Sephardi, her mother cooked very English foods. It wasn't until Martyne left home that she discovered how spices and herbs could transform food into something that delights and surprises. A love affair had begun.

Fortunately for Martyne, others liked her food, too, and she was able to change a hobby into a successful catering business. You can see more about Martyne's business at www.thecookingcrew.com

Linda Dangoor

Linda Dangoor was born in Baghdad, Iraq. She is a designer, painter and potter, and now also a food writer. She has worked in the design field for many years, creating and manufacturing products for the gift market in Paris and London.

Linda is the author of a cookbook entitled *Flavours of Babylon*, in which she explores and celebrates the flavours and recipes of her Baghdadi heritage. You can follow her on Instagram at @lindadangoorcreativeliving and Twitter at @lindadangoor or visit www.lindadangoor.com

Michael Daniel

Michael Daniel and his brother Daniel opened the first The Gate restaurant in the UK in 1989 when vegetarian food in restaurants was a niche concept. Thirty years on, the Iraqi-Indian Jewish brothers have a reputation as 'plant-based pioneers' and run four The Gate restaurants in London's Marylebone, Angel, Hammersmith and St John's Wood. They have also published two cookbooks. You can visit The Gate at www.thegaterestaurants.com or follow the restaurants on Instagram and Twitter at @GateRestaurant

Rachel Davies

With a degree in Theology and no culinary ability whatsoever, Rachel's passion for cooking started while on VSO in Zambia. Having never cooked before, she was forced to learn fast while living in a village with no supermarket. So, she started baking her own bread, making granita using lemons from her garden, and searching for recipes wherever she could find them, and the rest, as they say, is history.

After graduating in Cuisine and Patisserie from Le Cordon Bleu, Rachel went on to work with some of London's most inspiring chefs at Galvin Bistro de Luxe in Baker Street, Lanka Patisserie in Primrose Hill, and Divertimenti Cookery School.

In 2010, Rachel started Rachel's Kitchen as a way to share her passion for great food using quality ingredients. Over the past decade, Rachel has taught thousands of people the confidence to create delicious dishes in the kitchen. She is a judge for the Great Taste Awards and the Quality Food Awards, and is a member of the Dames D'Escoffier.

You can follow Rachel on Instagram at @rachelskitchenuk and Twitter at @RachDavies or visit www.rachels-kitchen.com

Aviva Elias

Aviva Elias was born and raised in Singapore and she had her eyes and tastes open to an abundance of cuisines from a young age. Ever curious, she ventured across five continents tasting and learning how best to combine flavours, colours and textures. She brought these together in Saffron, catering events in the UK and afar for over 20 years, including a brief sojourn back in Singapore catering for the Jewish community where she grew up. You can follow her on Instagram at @avivaelias

Michelle Eshkeri

Michelle Eshkeri opened Margot Bakery in East

Finchley, North London in 2016, specialising in sourdough pastries and bread. Born in Manchester and raised in Australia, she has lived in London for 20 years. You can follow her on Instagram and Twitter at @margotbakery or visit www.margotbakery.co.uk

Paola Gavin

Paola Gavin is a food writer and author of four vegetarian cookbooks on Italian, French, Mediterranean and Jewish food. She is also one of the contributors to *The 100 Most Jewish Foods*. Her latest book is *Hazana: Jewish Vegetarian Cooking* which features traditional Jewish dishes from around the world. She has also contributed to various publications including *The Gourmand*, *The Guardian* and *The Woodstock Times*. Many of her recipes can be found on Instagram at @paolagavin and on Twitter at @paolagavinfood

Lisa Goldberg and The Monday Morning Cooking Club

You can follow them on Instagram at @MondayMorningCC, Monday Morning Cooking Club on Facebook or visit https://mondaymorningcookingclub.com.au

Lisa Goldberg is a self-confessed fresser with an unbridled passion for eating, cooking and nurturing those around her with food. Her legal background has given her a great foundation to guide the Monday Morning Cooking Club sisterhood to produce and publish four extraordinary cookbooks. Since 2006 she has been completely dedicated to their delicious, inspiring and worthwhile project.

Oren Goldfeld

Hailing from Israel, with its extraordinary contemporary food scene, Chef Oren delivers equally extraordinary flavours. His first stint in the UK at Yotam Ottolenghi's Nopi was followed by the role of Head Chef at Restaurant 1701, Britain's first fine-dining restaurant celebrating Jewish cuisine. Acclaimed as the world's number one kosher restaurant, thanks to Oren's unique interpretation of a thousand years of culinary tradition, Restaurant 1701 was listed in the Michelin Guide within four months of opening. He then went on to launch several other restaurants. You can follow him on Instagram at @oren_g_chef

Gabrielle Rossmer Gropman and Sonya Gropman

Gabrielle Rossmer Gropman is a visual artist and mediation professional, who was born in Germany in 1938 and emigrated to the United States in 1939. Her art has been exhibited throughout the United States as well as in Germany. A multimedia art installation about the history of her German-Jewish family was exhibited at the Villa Dessauer Municipal Museum in the town of her birth, Bamberg, Gemany, in 1991 and again in 2013–14. You can follow her on Instagram at @cootegerjewcuisine

Sonya Gropman, her daughter, is a painter, photographer and writer whose work has been exhibited and published in the United States. She is involved in local sustainable agriculture in New York City. She and Gabrielle co-author the website germanjewishcuisine.com, where they post original material about German-Jewish food and culture. Their Twitter handle is @Ger_Jew_Cuisine or visit www.germanjewishcuisine.com. Their Facebook page is facebook.com/GermanJewishCuisine

Gil Hovav

Gil Hovav is an Israeli author, restaurant critic and TV presenter. He never studied cooking but has published ten cookbooks, and he really dislikes sushi. You can follow him on Instagram at @gilhovavisrael

Clarissa Hyman

Clarissa Hyman is a food and travel writer who has contributed to a wide range of national and international publications. She has twice won the prestigious Glenfiddich Food Writer of the Year Award and has published five books: *The Jewish Kitchen*, *The Spanish Kitchen* and *Cucina Siciliana*, plus books on the global history of oranges and the tomato. A former vice-president of the Guild of Food Writers in the UK, Clarissa is based in Manchester, England. You can follow her on Instagram at @hymanclarissa

Judy Jackson

Judy Jackson was originally a translator before starting a small catering business. This led to her giving cookery classes and the publication of the first of many cookbooks. She went on to write two novels and a memoir, but continued writing about food in the form of a food blog, which has over 3000 posts.

Now she also has a video channel (YouTube: Kitchen Games). You can follow her on Twitter at @judythewriter or visit thearmchairkitchen.com

Adam Kendler

Adam Kendler started making fudge in 2015, partly out of curiosity for such a magical sweet treat and also due to ordering what looked like delicious fudge online but which ended up tasting like rubber! Adam spent hours researching different methods and experimented with various recipes, then finally tweaked his own take on non-traditional, all-natural, soft and creamy fudge that melts in the mouth. You can follow him on Instagram at @artizanfudge or visit artizanfudge.co.uk

Leah Koenig

Leah Koenig's writing and recipes have appeared in *The New York Times*, *New York Magazine*, *The Wall Street Journal*, *The Washington Post*, *Epicurious*, *Food52*, *Departures*, and *Tablet*, among other publications. Leah is the author of six cookbooks including *The Jewish Cookbook* (Phaidon, 2019) and *Modern Jewish Cooking* (Chronicle Books, 2015). In addition to writing, Leah also leads cooking demonstrations and workshops around the world. She lives in Brooklyn, New York, with her husband and two children. You can follow her on Instagram at @leah.koenig and Twitter at @leahbkoenig or visit www.leahkoenig.com

Kim Kushner

Kim Kushner is a teacher and the author of three bestselling cookbooks: *I ♡ Kosher*, *The New Kosher* and *The Modern Menu*. Raised in Montreal, Canada, Kim learned to cook at an early age from her Moroccan-born mother and spent summers with family in Israel. She has become well known for her healthy and hearty dishes made from locally grown produce – not necessarily the first thing that comes to mind when thinking of kosher cuisine.

Kim has appeared on The Today Show (NBC) and has been featured in *The Huffington Post*, *Saveur* and *The Chicago Tribune*. Kim lives in New York City with her husband and four children. You can follow her on Instagram at @kimkushnercuisine and Twitter at @kimkushcuisine or visit kimkushner.com

Amy Lanza

Divine Chocolate is a global, farmer-owned chocolate company. They use the amazing power of chocolate to delight and engage. They bring people together to create dignified trading relations, empowering both producers and consumers. You can follow Amy Lanza (who contributed the recipe to this cookbook – Nourishing Amy for Divine Chocolate) on Instagram and Twitter at @nourishing.amy or visit nourishingamy.com

David Lebovitz

David Lebovitz is a professional chef and author. He launched www.davidlebovitz.com in 1999 to coincide with the launch of his first book, *Room for Dessert*. Twenty years later, he was honoured by *Saveur* magazine with their first-ever Blog of the Decade award. He is the author of nine books and lives in Paris. You can follow David on Instagram and Twitter at @davidlebovitz or visit www.davidlebovitz.com

Silvia Nacamulli

Silvia Nacamulli is a London-based cook and well-recognised name on the international food and cooking circuit. She grew up in Rome, surrounded by her home country's passion for food and today specialises in authentic Italian Jewish cuisine. She runs Cooking for the Soul, where she teaches and caters traditional home-cooking. Silvia regularly contributes recipes for *The Jewish Chronicle* and she is currently writing her first book, *Jewish Flavours of Italy*. You can follow her on Instagram @Silvia_Nacamulli or visit www.cookingforthesoul.com

Joan Nathan

Joan Nathan was born in Providence, Rhode Island, US, and is a Jewish-American cook and journalist. A frequent contributor to *The New York Times* as well as other publications, Joan is also the author of an impressive total of 11 cookbooks that span her four-decade-long career, including the James Beard and IACP award-winning titles, *Jewish Cooking in America* and *The New American Cooking*.

Joan is an avid collector of recipes belonging to the worldwide Jewish diaspora, having travelled to countries like France and Brazil for research, and her cookbooks are just as filled with fascinating history titbits as they are with wonderful recipes. Ever interested in sharing Jewish food with the world, she is also a co-founder of New York's Ninth Avenue

Food Festival, and divides her time between Washington D.C. and Martha's Vineyard in the US. You can follow her on Instagram and Twitter at @Joan_Nathan or visit joannathan.com

Sarit Packer

Sarit Packer and Itamar Srulovich are the chefs behind Middle Eastern restaurants Honey & Co and Honey & Smoke and food shop Honey & Spice, all in the neighbourhood of Fitzrovia, London, UK. The couple also write a column for the *FT Weekend Magazine*, host a podcast Honey & Co: The Food Talks, and have written four cookbooks. Their latest cookbook, *Chasing Smoke: Cooking Over Fire Around the Levant*, was published by Pavilion Books in May 2021. You can follow Sarit and Honey & Co on Instagram and Twitter at @honeyandco or visit honeyandco.co.uk

Denise Phillips

Denise Phillips is a British Jewish chef and author of seven cookbooks and numerous newspaper and magazine columns. As well as creating new recipes, she runs 'hands-on' classes and has used cookery for her Date On A Plate matchmaking for the last 16 years. Her latest recipes are available on her Instagram at @denises_kitchen. For more information visit www.jewishcookery.com or you can follow Denise on Twitter at @jewishcookery

Dr. Claudia Prieto Piastro

Dr. Claudia Prieto Piastro is a food anthropologist; her works focuses on the role of food in the construction of national identity. Since 2018, she has been a lecturer at LBIC/Brunel University of London where she teaches modules on Social Sciences and Intercultural Studies. You can follow her on Instagram at @piastromexicankitchen

Victoria Prever

Victoria Prever has been the food editor at *The Jewish Chronicle* for the past ten years. Before that, she left a legal career to follow her first love (food) and train as a professional chef at Leith's School of Food and Wine in the UK. She also contributes to *Olive* and *Good Food* magazines in the UK, and teaches cookery as well as working as a food consultant.

Victoria has appeared on Channel 4's Sunday Brunch, on BBC 1's Sunday Morning Live, as well as on BBC News digital in the UK. You can follow her on Instagram at @victoriaprever and Twitter at @YummierMummy or visit https://thejc.com/fresser

Rabbi Deborah R. Prinz

Rabbi Deborah Prinz is the author of *On the Chocolate Trail: A Delicious Adventure Connecting Jews, Religions, History, Travel, Rituals and Recipes into the Magic of Cacao*. The book forms the foundation for a museum exhibit, *Semite Sweet: On Jews and Chocolate*. She is the co-author with Tami Lehman-Wilzig of a children's picture book, *The Boston Chocolate Party*, which will be published in October 2022. You can follow her on Facebook at Deborah Prinz, Instagram at @chocolatetrail and Twitter at @deborahprinz or visit www.onthechocolatetrail.org

Rosalind Rathouse

Rosalind Rathouse is a professional cook who founded Cookery School in central London in 2003 after having taught cookery for many years in both England and her native South Africa. You can follow her on Instagram at @cookeryschoollondon and Twitter at @cookeryschool or visit www.cookeryschool.co.uk

Estee Raviv

Estee Raviv was born on the sandy shores of the Mediterranean. She was influenced by flavours of the Middle East, along with her Jewish heritage and the Eastern European traditions of her Romanian mother – an incredible cook and hostess – and Polish father. Estee is a vegan author and blogger. She is the author of *Oy Vey Vegan*, and she has been featured in many publications, most notably *VOGUE* magazine and *Vegan Life Magazine UK*. You can follow her on Instagram at @fromesteeskitchen and on Facebook at www.facebook.com/FromEsteesKitchen or visit www.esteeskitchen.com

Claudia Roden

Claudia Roden was born in Cairo and now lives in London. She is a critically-acclaimed food writer with a special interest in the cultural, social and historical background of food, exemplified in *The Book of Jewish Food: An Odyssey from Samarkand and Vilna to the Present Day*. Her other works include *Arabesque*, *The Food of Italy*, *Tamarind & Saffron* and *The Food of Spain*.

Judi Rose

Judi Rose is the daughter of legendary food writer and doyenne of Anglo-Jewish cookery, the late Evelyn Rose, MBE. They wrote numerous articles and two cookbooks together, including *The First Time Cookbook* while Judi was a student at Cambridge University. Following a career at the BBC, Judi moved to New York, where she taught international cooking and culinary techniques. Her most recent book, *To Life! Healthy Jewish Food*, was published in 2020. Judi nows runs The Cookery Studio, a boutique cookery school for all ages and skill levels in West London. The Studio's emphasis is on cooking (and eating) as a fun, creative and delicious way to meet like-minded people and make new friends, or to host food-themed parties and events. www.judirose.com

Alan Rosenthal

A lifelong culinary creative, Alan Rosenthal created his own food brand Stewed! – a range of tasty, as-good-as-homemade stew pots in the UK. He runs cookery workshops with Leith's School of Food and Wine in the UK. His first cookbook was *Stewed! Nourish your Soul*, and his latest book, *Foolproof One-pot*, was published in February 2021. You can follow him on Instagram at @alan.rosenthal and Twitter at @AlanRosenthal3 or visit www.alanrosenthal.co.uk

Leticia Moreinos Schwartz

Leticia Schwartz is a cookbook author, spokesperson and food reporter who is passionate about food and cooking, health and fitness, and culture and travel. She is a nationally recognised food personality in the US and frequently appears on major network programmes such as The Today Show (NBC), CT Live (NBC), Fox News, Sara's Weeknight Meals (PBS) and more.

As a food reporter, her work has been featured in a variety of web and print media outlets such as *The New York Times*, *Fine Cooking Magazine*, *Saveur*, *The Washington Post*, *Eating Well*, and more. She also teaches virtual cooking classes. You can follow her on Instagram at @leticiamoreinosschwartz and Twitter at @chefLeticia or visit chefleticia.com

Jenn Segal

Jenn Segal is a chef, cookbook author and blogger. Once upon a time she was a chef but left the restaurant business in 2003. A book agent told her in 2009 that she had no chance of having a cookbook published, so she started a blog instead. The agent was wrong – her first cookbook, called *Once Upon a Chef*, was published in 2018. You can follow her on Instagram and Twitter at @onceuponachef and www.onceuponachef.com

Paula Shoyer

Paula Shoya, The Kosher Baker, is the author of *The Healthy Jewish Kitchen*, *The Holiday Kosher Baker*, *The Kosher Baker*, *The New Passover Menu* and *The Instant Pot Kosher Cookbook*. Paula has a French pastry degree from Paris and does cooking events all around the world. She is a freelance writer, cookbook editor and brand ambassador for kosher food companies. Paula competed on Food Network's Sweet Genius and has appeared on TV over 45 times, including in Israel. Paula lives in Chevy Chase, Maryland, US. You can follow her on Instagram @kosherbaker and Twitter at @paulashoyer or visit thekosherbaker.com

Michael Solomonov

Michael Solomonov is a beloved champion of Israel's extraordinarily diverse and vibrant culinary landscape. With his business partner Steve Cook, Solomonov is co-owner of Philadelphia's CookNSolo Restaurants, which include Zahav, the trailblazing Israeli restaurant where Solomonov is chef. He is also the co-author of three cookbooks.

Solomonov is the recipient of five James Beard awards, including 2016 Book of the Year for his and Cook's bestseller *Zahav: A World of Israeli Cooking*, as well as 2017 Outstanding Chef, and 2019 Outstanding Restaurant for Zahav. *Food & Wine Magazine* recognised Zahav as one of the 2018 '40 Most Important Restaurants of the Past 40 Years'. You can follow him on Instagram at @mikesolomonov and Twitter at @mike_solomonov

Marlena Spieler

Marlena Spieler has been writing (and occasionally illustrating) award-winning cookbooks and food books for decades; her first (cook) book, *Naturally Good*, was published by Faber and Faber when she was still a teenager. Her nearly 70 cookbooks range wide in topics and include a series of Jewish cookbooks. She loves chocolate, but not nearly as much as her grandmother did, who ate it every day and worked full-time until she passed away aged 94. You can follow Marlena on Instagram and Twitter at @marlenaspieler or visit marlenaspieler.com

Emma Spitzer

Emma Spitzer was born and raised in Brighton to Jewish parents of Russian and Polish descent. Her love of cooking started at a very early age. Emma shadowed her mother in the kitchen as she regularly cooked Ashkenazi Jewish dishes passed down from her Polish parents.

Emma now loves to draw influences from her travels through the Middle East, her cultural heritage and her mother-in-law's North African roots. She creates food with lots of passion and lots of spice. Her debut cookbook *Fress: Bold Flavours from a Jewish Kitchen* was published in April 2017. You can follow Emma on Instagram and Twitter at @emmaspitzer or visit emmaspitzer.com

Adeena Sussman

Adeena Sussman is the author of *Sababa: Fresh, Sunny Flavors from my Israeli Kitchen* (published by Avery/Penguin Books, 2019), which was named a Best Fall 2019 cookbook by *The New York Times*, *Bon Appetit*, and *Food & Wine*. She is currently working on her follow up to *Sababa*, all about the foods of Shabbat.

The co-author of 14 cookbooks, Adeena's three most recent collaborations, including *Cravings* and *Cravings: Hungry For More* with Chrissy Teigen, were *The New York Times* best-sellers.

A lifelong visitor to Israel who has been writing about that country's food culture for almost 20 years, Adeena became a citizen in December 2018. She cooks and writes in Tel Aviv, Israel, where she lives in the shadow of the city's Carmel Market with her husband, Jay Shofet. Follow her on Instagram at @adeenasussman and Twitter at @adeenasussman or visit www.adeenasussman.com

Ofer Vardi

Ofer Vardi is a journalist and a foodie who can't keep his mouth shut. Based in Tel Aviv, Israel, Ofer grew up on his beloved grandmother's Hungarian cooking. Only after she passed away did he realise that the aromas of her delicacies had disappeared with her forever. Armed with a battered notebook of

recipes and his countless memories of Grandma Nana, Ofer embarked on his journey: to try and recreate the much-loved flavours of a time gone by. You can follow him on Instagram and Twitter at @ofervardi or visit ofervardi.com.ofer@lunch-box.co.il

Fabienne Viner-Luzzato

Fabienne is a French caterer and a cooking teacher with Tunisian and Italian origins who started Fabienne's Home Cooking in 2005. She is based in East Finchley, London, UK, and is known for her North African and Middle Eastern festive and generous tables. She also organises cooking lessons, demonstrations and parties for adults and children teaching various skills, from baking a cake or a tart to preparing a three-course meal from different cultures and tastes. You can follow her on Instagram at @fabienne_viner_luzzato and Twitter at @FabienneCooks or visit www.fabienneshomecooking.com

Jessie Ware and Lennie Ware

Table Manners: The Cookbook by Jessie Ware and Lennie Ware has been a success across the globe, with its collection of recipes that are delicious and suitable for cooks of all abilities. The cookbook is designed for busy people who want to create a family meal.

Jessie Ware is an award-winning English singer-songwriter, podcaster and author, who is currently working on her fourth record. She won Best New Voice at the 2018 Audio Production Awards for her successful podcast, Table Manners, which has hit more than eight million listens. You can follow her on Instagram at @tablemannerspodcast and Twitter at @JessieWare or visit https://smarturl.it/tablemanners

Lennie Ware is Jessie's mother and co-hosts Table Manners. The podcast has been touted 'hugely lovable', and continues to top the iTunes podcast chart. Lennie has worked as a social worker in family law for more than four decades. You can follow her on Instagram at @tablemannerspodcast and Twitter at @tablemannerspod or visit https://smarturl.it/tablemanners

Nino Shaye Weiss

After graduating from high school in Vienna in the 1980s, Nino Shaye Weiss moved to Paris and lived there for 12 years, where he studied art history and philosophy. In addition to studying for a doctorate, Nino worked as a cook, waiter and barman in the restaurant Zephyr in Paris. In search of himself and his Austro-Hungarian and Italian roots, Nino then took a 7-year detour via Yeshivah and Kollel in Bnei Brak, an ultra-orthodox suburb of Tel Aviv, Israel. There, together with his wife and children, he was able to get to know and live the religious laws and customs related to eating, cooking and baking.

Back again in Vienna, Nino founded and managed his website/blog, Jewish Viennese Food. Due to demand, Nino now offers cooking and baking classes, as well as gourmet tours through the city. Read more at http://JewishVienneseFood.com or check Instagram @jewishviennesefood or Twitter @NinoShayaWeiss

Sevim Zakuto

Sevim Zakuto trained as a kitchen manager and studied bakery and pastry before deciding to be her own boss. She loves coming up with new meal concepts at private events, or working with families and children at cookery classes. Sevim really enjoys bringing Middle Eastern and Turkish cuisine into her recipes, having grown up in Turkey and been trained by her grandmother in Turkish Sephardic food. You can follow her on Instagram at @realfood_by_sevimz

Orly Ziv

Orly Ziv is a nutritionist and cooking instructor from Tel Aviv, Israel. She is a culinary tour guide at www.cookinisrael.com. She has written several cookbooks, which draw on her Jewish-Greek heritage, and her recipes are full of Middle Eastern and Mediterranean flavours. You can follow Orly on Twitter at @CookinIsrael or visit cookinisrael.com

Text and Photograph Credits

Vegan Nutty Chocolate Chip Cookies extracted from Kenden Alfond's *The Jewish Food Hero Cookbook* (published by Jewish Lights, 2019).

The Gefilteria Dark Chocolate and Roasted Beet Ice Cream extracted from *The Gefilte Manifesto* by Liz Alpern & Jeffrey Yoskowitz. Copyright © 2016 Gefilte Manifesto LLC. Reprinted with permission from Flatiron Books. All rights reserved. Photography by Lauren Volo.

Chocolate-covered Cheese Confections extracted from *Please To The Table*, by Anya von Bremzen (published by Workman Pub. Co., 1990).

Curaçao Hot Chocolate and Panlevi extracted from *Recipes from the Jewish Kitchens of Curaçao* (first published by Drukkerij 'De Curaçaosche Courent' in 1982).

Sourdough Rye Brownies extracted from *Modern Sourdough: Sweet and Savoury Recipes* from Margot Bakery, by Michelle Eshkeri (published by White Lion Publishing, 2019).

Chocolate Hazelnut Cake extracted from *Hazana: Jewish Vegetarian Cooking* by Paola Gavin (published by Quadrille Books, 2017).

Spiced Chocolate Hazelnut Cookies (Krokerle) extracted from *The German Jewish Cookbook* by Gabrielle Rossmer Gropman and Sonya Gropman. New photography © Marc Gerstein. (published by Brandeis University Press, 2017).

Delicias aka Almond and Chocolate 'Delights' extracted from *The Spanish Kitchen* by Clarissa Hyman (published by Conran Octopus, 2005).

Chocolate-dipped Figs extracted from *Modern Jewish Cooking* by Leah Koenig (published by Chronicle Books, 2015).

Divine Chocolate Caramel Slices created by Amy Lanza (Nourishing Amy for Divine Chocolate).

Robert's Absolute Best Brownies extracted from *Ready For Dessert: My Best Recipes* [A Baking Book] by David Lebovitz, copyright © 2010, David Lebovitz. Used by permission of Ten Speed Press, an imprint of Random House, a division of Penguin Random House LLC. All rights reserved.

Chocolate and Marmalade Celebration Cake extracted from *Now for Something Sweet* (HarperCollins Australia, 2020; Text copyright © Monday Morning Cooking Club 2020; Photography copyright © Alan Benson 2020); recipe from Sydney matriarch and great-grandmother, Elza Levin.

Chocolate Almond Cake extracted from *Quiches, Kugels and Couscous* by Joan Nathan (published by Bravo Ltd., 2010).

Basque Chocolate Cake extracted from *On the Chocolate Trail: A Delicious Adventure Connecting Jews, Religions, History, Travel, Rituals and Recipes to the Magic of Cacao* (second edition), by Rabbi Deborah R. Prinz (published by Turner Publishing, 2017).

Rosalind Rathouse's Hazelnut Cake with Chocolate Ganache extracted from *The Gefiltefest Cookbook* (published by Grub Street, 2014).

Chocolate Pomegranate Discs, extracted from *To Life! Healthy Jewish Food* by Judi Rose & Dr Jackie Rose; Photography © Marc Gerstein

Acknowledgements

First and foremost – cooks, chefs and writers from around the world have donated wonderful, creative recipes. As well as contributing recipes, some have also tested the ideas of others and provided much-valued feedback.

Secondly, there are almost too many recipe testers to list. Again, their feedback has been extremely helpful. After some recipes, you'll see 'Tester's Tip', followed by the initials of the volunteer who made the suggestion.

Thank you to all these people: Nic Abery, Noga Applebaum, Karina Berger, Shana Boltin, Mekella Broomberg, Rebecca Daniels, Jessica Feather, Dan Friedman, Jane Graf, Neil Grayshon, Lauren Hamburger, Nicole Horowitz, Tonie Jascourt, Judianne Jayson, Laura Joseph, Fleur Just, Deborah Kahn-Harris, Susie Simmons Kaye, Tarryn Klotnick, Debby Konigsberg, Adrieen Kürti, Imogen Landy, Miri Lewis, Nick Mansfield, Fotini Marcopulos, Sheri Margolis, Julia Marcuson, Tammy Nisner, Judith Offman, Nicole Pragai, Andrew Risner, Ines Romanelli, Michelle Rose, Tracey Rosenfeld, Jo Rynhold, Noemi Schlosser, Miki Shaw, Daliah Sherrington, Corinne Shmuel, Matt Smoker-Mulhern, Deborah Sobel, Michael Stuart, Ruth Szotten, Julia Wagner, Nicki Witkin, and Annie Wigman.

Thirdly, Louise Hager, Jamie Herz, Lisa Steele and Caroline Tunkel at Chai Cancer Care, and all the Chai volunteers: Sharon Bearman, Jenni and Gary Colet, Elise Buckman, Carol Ellman, Diane Fenton, Julia Soning, Jackie Sharpstone, Karyn Orchant and Miriam Schajer.

For support in the UK, my thanks go to everyone at Pen & Sword Books, in particular Charles Hewitt for supporting this project, Tara Moran, Lori Jones, Sarah Guest, Rebecca Lawther and Peter Winfield. For sales in North America, I'm very grateful to David Farnsworth and his excellent team at Casemate Books.

Fourthly, the team that worked on every page of this book: Anne Sheasby worked tirelessly and thoroughly on every recipe; Julie Carpenter and Nicola Christie helped with the introductory text; Emma Pritchard and Laura Nickoll have proof-read all the text; Ian Hughes has worked his usual, admirable magic on the design of the front jacket and every page, Donald Sommerville has similarly been a great help on key texts and, finally, Judi Rose found perfect images and provided editorial and design advice from the word go, as well as a lovely chocolate recipe. Kayley Finegold and Marc Gerstein also provided important advice and ideas.

Finally, thanks to my wife Rachel – without whom I would have never become so involved in the world of Jewish food – and my wonderful sons, Sammy and Jack. They were dragged around countless chocolate shops and museums in Bayonne, France, as part of the research for this book and a story book, *The Chocolate King*. Through the Covid lockdown they watched this project develop and tasted some delicious (and a few not-so-delicious) baking efforts along the way.

Also available from Green Bean Books

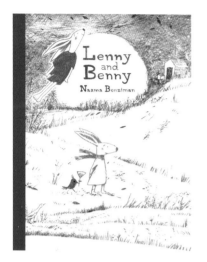

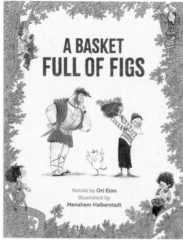

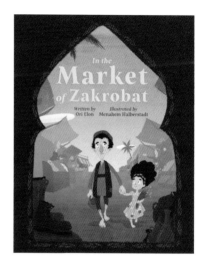

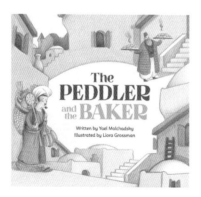

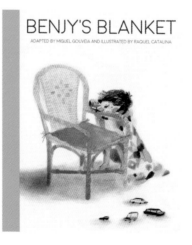

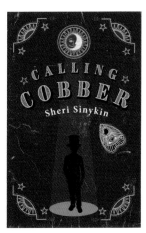

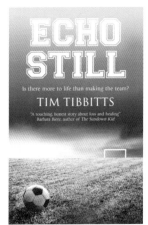

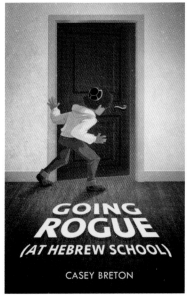

And finally

We need your help!
All sales of this book are raising money for Chai Cancer Care.
If you have enjoyed the collection, please post a review on Amazon,
or post a comment on Facebook, Instagram or Twitter.

Don't forget to tag Chai Cancer Care and Green Bean Books!

@green_bean_books
@chaicancercare